July 2004

We may not be
close in age but we're
close in heart.

"Hands across the crib railing
forever!"

Love,

Jan

Your Loving Sister

Your Loving Sister

a celebration of sisters through the ages

Edited by Laurel Hoffman

GRAMERCY BOOKS

NEW YORK

Keep It Together by Madonna Ciccone and Stephen Bray
© 1989 WB Music Corp., Blue Disque Music Co., Inc., Webo Girl Publishing, Inc. & Black Lion Music, Inc. All Rights o/b/o Webo Girl Publishing, Inc. & Blue Disque Music Co., Inc. administered by WB Music Corp. All Rights Reserved. Used by permission. WARNER BROS. PUBLICATIONS U.S. INC. Miami, FL 33014

This 2003 edition is published by Gramercy Books, an imprint of Random House Value Publishing, a division of Random House, Inc., New York, by arrangement with Career Press.

Gramercy is a registered trademark and the colophon is a trademark of Random House, Inc.

Random House
New York • Toronto • London • Sydney • Auckland
www.randomhouse.com

Printed and bound in Singapore

A catalog record for this title is available from the Library of Congress.

ISBN 0-517-22294-9

10 9 8 7 6 5 4 3 2 1

Contents

Acknowledgments *xi*
Introduction *xiii*

Acquiring a Beloved Babysitter   *Tatyana Tolstoy and her cousin Varya, 3*
Acquiring a Competitive Drive   *Diana Ross and her sister Barbara Jean, 5   /*
     Diana Princess of Wales and her sister Sarah, 6
Acquiring a Protector   *Carol Buckley and her sister Maureen, 9*
Admiring a Sister's Charm   *Nancy Langhorne Astor and her sister Irene, 11   /*
     Roseanne and her sister Geraldine Barr, 13   /   Anne Frank and her sister
     Margot, 14   /   Ava Gardener and her sister Myra Gardner Pearce, 15
Appraising a Sister's Fiancé   *Virginia Stephen Woolf and her future brother-*
     in-law Clive Bell, 18
Celebrating a Brother's Birthday   *Elizabeth Barrett Browning and her*
     brother Edward Barrett, 20
Celebrating a Brother's Engagement   *Lydia Jackson Emerson and her*
     brother Charles Jackson, 22
Celebrating the Sister-Brother Bond   *Madonna and her sisters Paula,*

Melanie, and Jennifer and her brothers Anthony, Christopher, Martin, and Mario Ciccone, 24 / William Wordsworth and his sister Dorothy, 26

Choosing Paths in Life   *Sylvia Ashton-Warner and her sister Daphne, 28 / Pauline Bonaparte and her brother Napoleon, 30*

Confiding About Ambition   *Florence Nightingale and her cousin Hilary Carter, 32*

Confiding About Health Problems   *Mary Todd Lincoln and her cousin Elizabeth Todd Grimsley, 35*

Confiding About Home Life   *Emily Dickinson and her brother William, 37 / Nancy Resedale Mitford and her brother Thomas, 38*

Confiding About Personal Danger   *Dolly Madison and her sister Anna, 40*

Confiding About Political Fears   *Mary Wollstonecraft Shelley and her brother-in-law Alexander Berry, 42*

Confiding About School   *Sylvia Plath and her brother Warren, 44*

Confiding About Work Frustration   *Maria Sklodowski Curie and her cousin Henrika Michalowska, 46 / Margaret Mitchell and her sister-in-law Frances Marsh, 47 / Harry Truman and his sister Mary, 49*

Consoling a Grieving Sister   *Louisa May Alcott and her sister Anna, 51*

Discussing Married Life   *Abigail May Alcott and her brother Samuel, 53 / Amelia Earhart and her sister, Muriel, 55 / Edith Jones Wharton and her sister Minnie, 56*

Encouraging Education   *Abigail Smith Adams and her sister Mary, 58 / Pat Ryan Nixon and her brother William Ryan, 59*

CONTENTS

Expressing Faith and Spiritual Contentment   *George Eliot (Mary Ann Evans) and her cousin Sarah Hennel, 62   /   Alice James and her brother William, 63*

Expressing Love and Gratitude   *Mary Baker Eddy and her brother George, 65   /   Katherine Beauchamp Mansfield and her brother Leslie, 66   /   Anna "Bamie" Roosevelt and her sister-in-law Edith Carrow Roosevelt, 68*

Imparting the Secrets of Success   *Katharine Meyer Graham and her sister Bis Meyer, 70*

Improving Writing Ability   *Caroline Darwin and her brother Charles Darwin, 72   /   Ellen Tucker Emerson and her brother Edward Emerson, 73*

Nurturing a Sick Brother   *Agnes Crane and her brother Stephen, 75   /   Ada Lawrence and her brother D. H. Lawrence, 77   /   Grandma Moses (Anna Mary Robertson) and her brother Fred, 78   /*

Offering Character Advice   *Susan B. Anthony and her sister Mary, 80   /   Maria Edgeworth and her brother Henry, 81   /   Golda Mabovitch Meir and her sister Shenya Mabovitch, 83*

Providing Career Encouragement   *Virginia Louise Meredith and her brother Burgess, 85*

Providing Emotional Support   *Sarah Muir and her brother John, 88   /   Mabel Wolfe and her brother Thomas, 89*

Providing Protection   *Clara Barton and her brother Stephen, 92   /   Marie Cuomo and her brother Mario, 94   /   Jane Fonda and her brother Peter, 96   /   Miriam and her brother Moses, 97   /   Phoebe Anne*

(Annie) Oakley and her brother John, 99 / Benjamin Spock and his sister Hiddy, 100 / Elie Wiesel and his sister Tsipouka, 102 / Natalie (Natasha Gurdin) Wood and her sister Lana, 104

Providing Reminiscences About Growing Up   *Izabela Walesa and her brother Lech, 106*

Rejoicing in Nostalgia   *E. B. White and his sister Marion, 108 / Katherine Beauchamp Mansfield and her sister Jeanne Beauchamp, 109*

Relating Exciting News   *Dorothy Dow and her sister Frances, 111*

Relating Motherly Joy   *Fanny Burney and her brother James, 113*

Remembering a Departed Brother   *Eleanor Roosevelt and her brother Hall, 115 / Sophie Thoreau and her brother Henry David, 116*

Remembering a Departed Sister   *Mary Hunter Austin and her sister Jennie, 118 / Margaret Fuller and her sister Julia, 120*

Sharing a Séance for a Departed Father   *Barbra Streisand and her brother Shelley, 122*

Sharing Childhood Affection   *Barbara Pierce Bush and her brother Scott Pierce, 125 / Frederick Douglass and his sisters Eliza and Sarah, 126 / Letty Konigsberg and her brother Woody Allen, 128 / Mia Farrow and her brother Michael, 129 / Buddy Foster and his sister Jodie, 131 / Maureen Reagan and her brother Michael, 133 / Iovanna Wright and her sister Svetlana, 135*

Sharing Companionship in Old Age   *Maja Einstein and her brother Albert, 137 / Annie Elizabeth (Bessie) Delaney and her sister Sarah Louise (Sadie), 139*

CONTENTS

Sharing Concern for an Ailing Mother   *Edna St. Vincent Millay and her sister Norma, 141*

Sharing Creative Hobbies and Interests   *Beatrix Potter and her brother Bertram, 143*

Sharing Family   Grief *Jane Austen and her brother Francis, 145*

Sharing Humor and Pranks   *Maya Henderson Angelou and her brother Bailey Henderson, 147 / Barry Goldwater and his sister Carolyn, 149 / Ruth Ann and Sally Schwarzkopf and their brother Norman, 150 / Eudora Welty and her brother Edward, 152*

Sharing Imaginative Play   *Jorge Luis Borges and his sister Norah, 154 / Jane Bowles and her cousin Mary Jane Shour, 156 / Sarah (Fergie) Ferguson and her sister Jane, 158 / Kate Greenaway and her sister Fanny, 159 / Vanessa Redgrave and her brother Corin, 161*

Sharing Musical Activities   *Elisabeth Jolley and her sister Karen, 163*

Sharing Stimulating Conversation   *Simone de Beauvoir and her sister Louise (Poupette), 165*

Sharing Theatrical Play   *Lucille Ball and her brother Freddy, 167 / Charlotte Bronte and her sisters Anne and Emily, and her brother Branwell, 168*

Sibling Rivalry   *Vanessa Stephen Bell and her sister Virginia Woolf, 171 / Jacqueline Kennedy Onassis and her sister Lee Bouvier Radziwill, 172*

Teaching the Art of Storytelling   *Helena Petrovna Blavatsky and her sister Vera, 174 / Agatha Christie and her sister Madge, 176*

Teaching Boldness   *Shana Alexander and her sister Laurel, 178 / Peter (Cohon) Coyote and his sister Elizabeth Cohon, 179*

CONTENTS

Teaching Cooperation   *Heather Whitestone, and her sisters Melissa and Stacey, 181*

Teaching to Fight Prejudice   *Margaret Thatcher and her sister Muriel, 183*

Teaching Independent-Mindedness   *David Brinkley and his sister Margaret, 185   /   Theodore Dreiser and his sister Janet, 187*

Teaching a Life Hobby   *Josefine Freud and her sister Anna, 189*

Teaching Responsibility to Others   *Cesar Chavez and his sister Rita, 191*

Traveling Together   *Mary Kennedy Fisher and her sister Anne, 193*

Welcoming a New Sister-in-Law Into the Family   *Christina Rossetti and her sister-in-law Lucy Brown Rossetti, 195*

References   *197*

Acknowledgments

This book would scarcely have been possible without the valuable help of many people. The initial idea came from my literary agent, Alice Fried Martell, who was instrumental in bringing this project to the attention of editor Monica Harris; it has been a delight in working with Monica. For their conceptual contributions, I'm much indebted to my brother David, and his wife, Jackie, and particularly to my sister, Eleanor. As a former teacher, my mother offered a variety of helpful suggestions from the outset. In a real way, the medical patients and families I've worked with professionally over the past twenty years have taught me much about the importance of sisters during health, illness, and the vicissitudes of life.

On the home front, I wish to thank three individuals for their boundless encouragement. My children, Aaron and Jeremy, by often insisting that I take a break, helped me to stay cheerful and balanced—and to put "motherly wisdom" into challenging daily practice. My husband, Edward, more than any other person, gave me the emotional support to complete the project and fulfill my own expectations for it.

Introduction

Being a sister, and having a sister, have been vital to my life. With a chronically ill father (who died when I was nine) and a mother who worked long hours as a businesswoman to support us, I had the nearly constant companionship of my sister and brother. For fun, we'd play endless rounds of pinochle and challenging board games including Scrabble and Monopoly. Ice-skating outdoors on a frozen pond and swimming were our favorite sports.

But growing up, of course, wasn't endless play. Looking back on those early years, I can easily see how our activities together taught me valuable lessons about sharing, compromise, and negotiation. Having an older sister also gave me a role-model for clothing and style, and helped develop my social skills. By the time I was eight, I took pride not only in taking accurate phone messages for my teenage sister, but in skillfully fielding her callers as she sat doing homework in the living room. My brother and I inhabited different worlds back then, but without him I'd have known a lot less about the mysterious world of boys and their interests.

Later, as a teenager in the Vietnam War era, I began having serious conversations with my siblings about politics, social injustice, and career goals. Because my brother and sister were several years older, I became interested in societal matters by my early high-school years, and helped organize my peers to support the anti-war activities occurring at local colleges. I especially remember when I traveled with my siblings overnight from our Michigan neighborhood to attend a national protest rally in Washington, D.C.

Decades have passed since that time in our lives; and now, as a mother, wife, and professional social worker, I find my activities very different from those of our midwestern childhood. Following family and work trajectories, we're no longer residing in the same geographic region of the United States. Yet, my sisterly dialogue still flourishes in both familiar and new ways.

After recently completing *The Book of Mothers' Wisdom,* I was eager to undertake a new project. Roaming far and wide in history to amass inspiring, maternal guidance for that book had been fascinating, and to focus next on sisters seemed appealing to me. I knew the topic held a lot of interest nowadays, and was also one on which comparatively little had been written. Certainly, from my twenty-year career as a medical social worker, I'd come to appreciate the supportive, care-giving role of sisters when families are faced with a serious illness. This was a facet of social life that I encountered in my childhood, through the efforts of both my sister and my mother's two sisters of her own.

Far more broadly, though, than simply looking at caregiving, I wanted to see how history's celebrated women had experienced sisterhood: what did they most cherish or extol? What was most endearing? Was it a force potent mainly in childhood, or rather, did it exert lifelong impact? What insecurities did the sisters ease and what fears could these sisters only confess to their sibling? What could siblings only disclose to their sisters? Aside from providing emotional or even physical nurturance during a family member's illness, what kinds of help did influential women like Louisa May Alcott, Amelia Earhart, or Barbra Streisand offer as sisters? How did sisterhood affect their achievements in art, education, literature, music, politics, or science?

Exploring such questions for *Your Loving Sister* has been exciting. As my research expanded, I decided to include not only historically famous women from Miriam of the Bible to popular contemporaries like Madonna, but also the little-known sisters of those who came to be renowned. For in many instances, they were cherished sources of affection, creativity, and courage—and sometimes (no less importantly) served as foils for self-assertion, ambition, and competitive drive. Thus, we see in a new light figures like Pauline Bonaparte, Caroline Darwin, Maja Einstein, Mary Truman, Muriel Thatcher, and many other women seemingly placed on history's sidelines. In a few instances, I've also included letters or anecdotes involving women such as Marie Curie, Mary Todd Lincoln, and Tatyana Tolstoy—speaking in sisterly fashion—to their cousins.

After reading hundreds of memoirs, autobiographies, collections of letters, and biographies to create this anthology, I'm more convinced than ever: sisterhood is among life's most beautiful bonds. My literary bounty clearly shows that sisters have not only been vital through the centuries as a source of guidance, consolation, and advice—but perhaps also for their sheer affection, sharing of experience, and caring interest—qualities that appear increasingly important and celebratory as we get older.

As young Emily Dickinson, feeling lonely in Amherst, reminded her brother Austin, who was away at college, "Home is a holy thing...I feel it more and more as the great world goes on." Or, as the English writer Katherine Mansfield, vacationing in a Swiss chalet more than a half-century later, nostalgically penned her younger sister: "Ah, Jeanne, anyone who says to me, 'Do you remember?' simply has my heart. Come off with me for a whole day—will you? And let's just remember."

If the wide-ranging selection in *Your Loving Sister* succeeds in re-kindling your own memories of sisterly camaraderie and warmth, advice and protection—or just plain fun and good times—then my hopes will have been fulfilled.

Your Loving Sister

Acquiring a Beloved Babysitter

·-·-·-·-·-

Tatyana Tolstoy and her cousin Varya

The Russian writer Leo Tolstoy ranks among the world's most highly regarded authors of enduring literature. The author of *War and Peace, Anna Karenina,* and other novels was also an important moralist, religious thinker, and social reformer. Tolstoy was a distinguished soldier during the Crimean War, then retired from military service in 1856. During the next few years, Tolstoy made several trips to western Europe, where he took a keen interest in educational methods. After returning to his estate, he opened a school for peasant children there.

Tolstoy was a progressive educator who believed that teaching should be adapted to the needs of each youngster. In a happy marriage later marked by turmoil, Leo Tolstoy and his wife, Sonya Behrs, raised five children. In *Tolstoy Remembered,* their eldest daughter, Tatyana, warmly recalled an important childhood friendship:

> ...I remember very well...my cousin Varya, the daughter of my

aunt, the Countess Marya Nicolayena Tolstoy....Once, her mother sent her to [live with us] to forget a man she was in love with and wanted to marry. I saw her weeping on more than one occasion, and I remember as though it were yesterday the feeling of love and compassion I experienced as I sat on her lap and leaned my head against her breast.

Varya was a wonderful storyteller. I have never heard droller stories than the ones she told us in the evenings then sitting in the half-dark on the big divan.

Our [governess] Hannah sometimes used to go on visits to her sister...it was on such occasions that Varya used to come down and sleep with us in the vaulted room.

Before leaving, Hannah would give Varya instructions about how to deal with us: what was allowed and what wasn't. Every night, when she tucked us into bed, it was Hannah's custom to give us each a little piece of licorice, which we loved. Varya was therefore issued with a large, round stick of licorice from which she was to slice off a tiny roundel for each of us every evening. To my great shame I must admit to such greediness that even today, more than fifty years later, I can still recall the pleasure with which I received from Varya a lump of licorice so large that Hannah would have made it last five or six evenings at the least. But my pleasure was short-lived: I couldn't manage to finish this oversized treat, which eventually began to make me feel sick. And I was so sleepy by then that I simply took it out of my mouth and surreptitiously dropped it on the floor, behind my bed.

Acquiring a Competitive Drive

* * * * * *

Diana Ross and her sister Barbara Jean

Diana Ross, a superstar in today's entertainment world, grew up in a lower-middle class family in 1950s Detroit. Showing early talent, she became lead singer for the female trio known as the Supremes and by her early twenties was one of Motown Records' most successful performers. Diana went solo in 1969 and immediately gained new hits with "Someday, We'll be Together," "Reach out and Touch Somebody's Hand," and "Ain't No Mountain High Enough." As an actress, her popular movies have included *Lady Sings the Blues* (portraying singer Billie Holiday) and *Mahogany*. Through live and televised concerts, Diana Ross has retained an enthusiastic following.

In a memoir entitled *Secrets of a Sparrow,* she recalled a key childhood influence:

> Barbara Jean was the first [born in the Ross family]. I thought she was the true beauty of the family. We called her Bobbi. I remember

loving her, wanting her touch and her warmth, my big sister. She had long pretty hair, she was very smart, and she wore glasses.

I was the second child, so as I got older, I was always competing with her. I could sing and dance better than she could. I was stronger, and....I could run really fast. I loved to swim. I remember Mama would come to watch me swim, and she used to think I looked pretty in the water because everybody else would be gasping for their breath, and I would just stroke smoothly along....I wanted my parents to like me as much as they liked [Bobbi]. I thought they liked her best, so I would do other things to get their attention. I'd try to entertain the family and see if I could bring a little joy into their lives, especially when I knew that they were unhappy.

I would try to do everything the best, better than Bobbi, so Mama and Daddy could see me. I was never afraid to stand up to my mother's friends and entertain them. Do a little tap dance or even sing *Your Cheatin' Heart.*

Diana, Princess of Wales and her sister Sarah

In her short, tumultuous life, Diana, Princess of Wales came to be one of the world's most popular and admired women. Though bright and attractive, she suffered bouts of low self-esteem from an early age. It was only before her tragic death in August 1997, that the princess seemed to develop a comfortable confidence in herself. Yet Diana's life was marked by an intense drive for achievement and influence.

In *Diana, Her True Story,* biographer Andrew Morton recounted that Diana, while growing up, venerated her two older sisters, Jane and Sarah:

> Doubtless there was discussion in the teachers' common room about which sister the latest Spencer recruit to Poplar class would emulate, Sarah or Jane. Diana's inevitable inclination was to imitate Sarah....In an attempt to copy her sister Sarah's exploits she accepted a challenge which nearly got her expelled. One evening her friends, reviewing the dwindling stocks of sweets in their tuck boxes, asked Diana to rendezvous with another girl at the end of the school drive and collect more supplies from her....[Diana accepted the dare.] As she walked down the treelined road in the pitch black, she managed to suppress her fear of the dark. When she reached the school gate, she discovered that there was no-one there. She waited....When two police cars raced in through the school gates, she hid behind a wall. Then she noticed the lights going on all over the school, but thought no more about it.
>
> Finally Diana returned to her dorm, terrified not so much at the prospect of getting caught, but because she had come back empty-handed. As luck would have it, [a classmate was ill]. As she was being examined, Diana's teacher noticed the empty bed. The game was up.

It was not just Diana who had to face the music but her parents as well....Secretly Diana's parents were amused that their dutiful but docile daughter had displayed such spirit. "I didn't know you had it in you," said her mother afterwards.

Acquiring a Protector

❖❖❖❖❖❖

Carol Buckley and her sister Maureen

Carol Buckley was born into the rich, influential American Irish-Catholic family that produced commentator-author William F. Buckley Jr. and former New York State Senator James Buckley. The youngest of ten children, she grew up with servants and foreign travel. The Buckleys, whose income came from oil, lived in Connecticut, South Carolina, Mexico, and Europe. At the age of forty-three, after struggling for years with alcoholism, Carol quit the empty life of a New York City socialite and went back to school—earning a degree in clinical social work before settling into a satisfying career as a counselor.

In her memoir, *At the Still Point,* Carol Buckley recalled:

> Maureen was six years older than I, and quite my opposite. She was serious, honest, funny, and very modest. Where I was devious, she was direct; where I was cowardly, she was brave. She didn't seem

overly fond of me in those days....But if she didn't seem to like me much then, she was ferocious in her protectiveness, and I learned during that year in Mexico that I could always, always count on her.

When the Buckleys lived in Mexico, Carol attended nursery school for one day, and was apprehensive. Her favorite toys were *Snow White and the Seven Dwarfs.* She found the mood unfriendly and authoritarian. One day during rest time, she put the beloved toys aside, and then headed for home.

When we were almost home, just across the street from our front door, I put my hands into the pockets of my coat and—they were gone! My Snow White! My dwarfs! I was disconsolate.

"Well, now"—that was all Maureen needed to hear. The next morning with [our nanny] Felipa holding one hand and Maureen the other, I was marched back to school, and Maureen who hated speaking Spanish and always pretended she didn't know how, unleashed a torrent of indignant reproaches. I do believe she used the word *ladrones*—thieves, brigands! And that very day, before school was over, Snow White and her dwarfs were returned to me by a very subdued teacher.

I don't know how she retrieved them, but I do know that I never had to go back to the play school again. What a victory! What a wonderful thing to have a sister Maureen!

Admiring a Sister's Charm

Nancy Langhorne Astor and her sister Irene

Raised in small-town Virginia, Nancy Langhorne went to England in 1903, and three years later married Waldorf Astor, a great-great-grandson of the wealthy American merchant John Jacob Astor. When her husband gave up his seat in the British House of Commons in 1919, Nancy was elected to replace him: the first woman ever to hold such office. A decade later, Nancy Astor unsuccessfully tried to create a women's party in the House under her leadership, and eventually retired from politics after a thirty-year career. She was known as a witty champion on behalf of women and children. Among her famous aphorisms: "The main dangers in life are the people who want to change everything—or nothing" and "The penalty of success is to be bored by the people who used to snub you."

As related in Christopher Sykes' biography, *Nancy, the Life of Lady Astor,* Lady Astor in a 1951 manuscript wrote lovingly of her sister Irene:

While Irene was still a schoolgirl, there were paragraphs in the papers, which used to annoy Father very much, saying a raving beauty was growing up in Richmond, Virginia, who would become the talk of the country. It was not then considered the thing to be talked about in the papers, and I remember when, later, one of them printed Irene's picture, Father threatened to go to New York and shoot the editor.

Irene wasn't only beautiful. She had wonderful charm. When she came in, it was like the sun streaming into the room. Nor did the praise and adulation she got ever go to her head. She remained entirely unspoiled and this was wonderful. Mostly she laughed at the fuss people made of her, and no doubt her brothers and sisters played their part in keeping her humble.

I remember once she came back from a visit where she had been the belle of every ball, and the papers had been full of flattering paragraphs about her...We all fell on her. "You may have looked beautiful at the party," we told her, "but people ought to see the way you look now."...She was the acknowledged family beauty, and none of us ever questioned it, and were quite satisfied to be the beautiful Irene Langhorne's sisters.

Roseanne and her sister Geraldine Barr

Actress and director Roseanne is best known for the long-running television sitcom that bore her name. Its portrait of working-class life came partly from her own experience. Growing up a Jewish outcast in the strict Mormon society of Salt Lake City, Utah, Roseanne had a difficult time. As a teenager in the 1960s, she had a terrifying near-death experience and was placed in a mental institution. She became a mother at an early age and was a member of the working poor. Determined, she ultimately succeeded as a stand-up comedienne in the 1980s, and finally broke through into television, hosting several specials and series and starring in her own show, *Roseanne,* beginning in 1988.

In *My Sister Roseanne,* Geraldine Barr looked back affectionately on their early years.

My first direct memory of my older sister, Roseanne, was when she poked pins in my head...As the story was explained to me when I was older, Rosey sat down with me when I was barely a toddler and placed ribbons on my hair. Then, instead of using a bobby pin... Rosey jabbed a hat pin straight down into my scalp. It was a technique that worked with dolls, teddy bears, and other stuffed toys. Certainly, she assumed, it would work with a baby sister.

Despite that rather harsh experience at the hands of my sister, I adored Rosey. She was my first playmate, my first best friend. My mother told me that when Rosey started school, I was so devastated that I sat on my couch, looking out the window, waiting for her to return. There were days when I sat like that for hours.

In my child's mind, I suppose that Rosey was the most mature young woman I could ever imagine encountering. She did not need diapers. She could tie her shoelaces. She had a fairly full set of teeth in her mouth. And she spent a lot of time playing with me.

Anne Frank and her sister Margot

The Diary of Anne Frank is among the world's most widely read works relating to the Holocaust and is celebrated in its own right for vividly depicting a teenage girl's struggle for self-identify. Anne Frank was born in Frankfurt, Germany, and relocated with her family to the Netherlands when Hitler came to power in 1933.

The *Diary* records the years between 1942 and 1944 that Anne and her family spent hiding—with the courageous assistance of non-Jewish friends—at a secret warehouse office-annex in Amsterdam. Later, they were discovered by Nazi officers acting on an informer's tip and deported to concentration camps.

Only Anne's father, Otto, survived. After World War II ended, he learned that family friends had found Anne's diary among papers left behind by German secret police. Published in 1947, the *Diary* has been translated into more than thirty languages. It movingly records her assertion that "In spite of everything, I still believe that people are really good at heart." Today the Frank family's hiding place on the Prinsengracht Canal in Amsterdam has become an international museum.

Anne often felt competitiveness regarding her sixteen-year-old sister Margot's place in the family. As a self-reflective thirteen-year-old, she observed:

> I love them; but only because they are Mummy and Margot. With Daddy it's different. If he holds Margot up as an example, approves of what she does, praises and caresses her, then something gnaws at me inside, because I adore Daddy. He is the one I look up to. I don't love anyone in the world but him. He doesn't notice that he treats Margot differently from me. Now Margot is just the prettiest, sweetest, most beautiful girl in the world. But all the same, I feel I have some right to be taken seriously too.
>
> I'm not jealous of Margot, never have been. I don't envy her good looks or her beauty. It is only that I long for Daddy's real love; not only as his child but for me—Anne, myself.

Ava Gardner and her sister Myra Gardner Pearce

Actress Ava Gardner is best remembered for her roles in now-classic movies like *Show Boat, The Bible,* and *The Night of the Iguana.* Other celebrated films include *The Snows of Kilimanjaro, The Barefoot Contessa,* and her Oscar-nominated performance opposite her screen idol, Clark Gable, in *Mogambo.*

Born on Christmas Eve, 1922, in rural North Carolina, Ava was the youngest of seven children. When she was two, her parents opened a boarding house for teachers at the rural Brogden School, and several years later, they operated another teacher's boarding house in the Rock Ridge community near Wilson township. Ava grew up as a pretty, risk-taking tomboy who was happiest running barefoot through the fields. During a visit to her older sister Beatrice and her photographer-husband Larry Tarr in New York City, Ava posed for photos. Larry displayed one in his studio window; it led to an MGM screen test and a movie contract in 1941. Beatrice went on to Hollywood with Ava and assisted in her skyrocketing career, with immensely publicized marriages to Mickey Rooney, bandleader Artie Shaw, and Frank Sinatra. At the age of thirty-three, Gardner moved to Madrid, Spain, and then settled in London—returning often to America for her film career and to visit relatives in rural North Carolina. Ava remained friendly with her ex-husbands and enjoyed a complex relationship with tycoon Howard Hughes. Though she never had children, she doted on her nieces and nephews.

In *Ava, My Story,* the renowned actress presented her sister Myra's reminiscence:

Because there were seven years between Ava and me, I guess a baby was not expected when she came along. Because of that, she was sort of special, and everybody did dote on her. She had naturally curly hair that Mama had to brush every morning before she'd go to school, [though] Ava always hated that...

Ava was sort of a tomboy, always climbing trees. When we lived over at Brogden, she got halfway up to the top of the town's water tank. Everybody was so frightened to see her up there. Finally, someone went up and got her down. Ava was a pretty little girl, too, and everybody thought she was so cute and wonderful, but to me she was just my baby sister.

We roomed together and we loved each other, but I never got the impression that she wanted to be in the movies. Mama loved to go to the movies, though, and she and some of the teachers from the teachers' residence would get together and go to Smithfield to see one most every week. Mama especially liked Clark Gable. I wish she could have lived long enough to know that Ava did a movie with him.

Appraising a Sister's Fiancé

━━━━━━

Virginia Stephen Woolf and her future brother-in-law Clive Bell

Virginia Woolf was a major British novelist, critic, and essayist. With acclaimed novels including *Mrs. Dalloway, To the Lighthouse,* and *Jacob's Room,* Virginia was a pioneer in stream-of-consciousness writing and a founding figure of the twentieth century's modernist literary movement. Born into an affluent London family, she was twenty-four years old when penning these bold words in October 1906 to her sister Vanessa's future husband:

> I can quite believe that you are very happy with Vanessa—but as she also seems to be very happy with you, I don't see that my sisterly solicitude has any right to complain. My friends take very good care that I shan't be lonely.
>
> [Nevertheless] I wish you would write a description of yourself—

your features, your gifts, your prospects, your parents—that I might know exactly who you are, and what you are, and above all, whether you are worthy of Vanessa. The general opinion seems to be that no one can be worthy of her; but as you are unknown, this is no reflection upon you. Only it will show you what kind of reputation she has; perhaps you know it already.

Celebrating a Brother's Birthday

━━━━━━

Elizabeth Barrett Browning and her brother Edward Barrett

Elizabeth Barrett Browning was one of Victorian England's most famous poets, with works including the romantically passionate *Sonnets From the Portuguese*. During her lifetime, Elizabeth came to be more admired for her literary talent than her poet-husband, Robert Browning.

Educated at home in classic Greek, Latin, and several modern languages, Elizabeth showed early genius, and, at the age of thirteen, published a long poem with her father's financial assistance. At the age of fifteen, she almost died from spinal injuries suffered in a fall and remained a semi-invalid throughout her life. When nearly forty and well-known in her own right, she met the poet Robert Browning in 1845, and the two married the following year. They eventually moved to Pisa and then Florence, Italy, where Elizabeth spent her final years, as a widow, writing poetry on social and political issues including the scourge of American slavery.

In June 1818, Elizabeth was only twelve years old when composing this celebratory poem to her brother Edward on his eleventh birthday:

> To sing no mighty deeds, I call the Muse
> To sweep those chords once more, I bid them swell
> In fainter notes to tell a Sister's love
>
> A brother's birth—Oh day, so dear, how oft
> The lyre unites her garland to the flowers
> Of liberal Nature's hand and joy completes!
>
> And, Oh, my brother, may the hand of heaven
> Preserve in happiness thy growing years!
>
> May truth and virtue guide thy steps to fame,
> May heaven in peace and joy prolong thy days!
>
> Years from thy life remorseless time has stolen
> With tenfold interest, years may he repay!

Celebrating a Brother's Engagement

━━━━━━

Lydia Jackson Emerson and her brother Charles Jackson

Lydia Jackson Emerson, the second wife of America's leading nineteenth-century philosopher, Ralph Waldo Emerson, was well-known for her wit and verbal eloquence. Born in Plymouth, Massachusetts, she and her two siblings were raised by relatives after their young mother died from tuberculosis. With a highly disciplined mind, Lydia was admirably self-taught, and together with eight women friends in Plymouth, she organized a Reading Society and issued a newsletter called *The Wisdom of the Nine*.

Lydia and Ralph Waldo Emerson married in 1835, four years after his first wife's death, and the year before his first book, *Nature,* was published to wide acclaim. From the outset, their mutual attraction was intense. Lydia shared her husband's mystical, poetic outlook on life, and became close with several of his friends including Henry David

Thoreau. She was a devoted mother, and as her four children entered their teenage years, Lydia's admonition was always: *common sense*. She is quoted, "Our confidence in you is entire, and there is no need to give you minute directions."

In 1833, Lydia's older brother, Charles, was studying medicine in Paris when she penned these congratulatory sentiments:

> I regard your engagement with high satisfaction, because, from what little I know of Susan personally, I should judge her to be possessed of such qualities as will secure you a large amount of domestic happiness. I very much admire Susan, as far as I have had an opportunity of observing her, and am confident that on a more intimate acquaintance, I shall find her all I could wish.
>
> You must tell Susan how well prepared I am to love her—for her own sake, as well as for yours. Should Providence permit your union, she shall find in me an affectionate sister and a devoted friend.

Celebrating the Sister-Brother Bond

—•••••••—

Madonna and her sisters Paula, Melanie, and Jennifer and her brothers Anthony, Christopher, Martin, and Mario Ciccone

Madonna is among the world's most popular entertainers. Her film credits include *Desperately Seeking Susan, Dick Tracy, Truth Or Dare,* and *Evita*. When she was twenty-five, she released her first album, *Madonna*. Since then, success has continued unabated. Her hit singles have included "Material Girl," "Live to Tell," "Papa, Don't Preach," "Express Yourself," and "You'll See." Her own label, Maverick Records, has also been a major success.

At age six, Madonna lost her mother, Madonna Fortin, due to breast cancer. With five siblings, Madonna's household was large and hard to manage, and her father married their housekeeper, Joan Gustafson, a few years later. Although she gained a dance scholarship to the University of Michigan, Madonna abruptly quit her studies, moved to New York City, and triumphed in her entertainment career goals.

In their powerful song "Keep It Together," written by Madonna and Stephen Bray, the popular singer offers these lines:

Keep, keep it together
Keep people together forever and ever

I got brothers, I got some sisters too
Stuck in the middle tell you what I'm gonna do
Gonna get out of here, I'm gonna leave this place
So I can forget every single hungry face
I'm tired of sharing all the hand me downs
To get attention I must always be the clown
I wanna be different, I wanna be on my own
But Daddy said listen, you will always have a home

Keep it together in the family
They're a reminder of your history
Brothers and sisters they hold the key
To your heart and your soul
Don't forget that your family is gold

I hit the big time but I still get the blues
Everyone's a stranger, city life can get to you
People can be so cold, never want to turn your back
Just givin' to get something
Always wanting something back

When I get lonely and I need to be
Loved for who I am, not for what they want to see
Brothers and sisters, they've always been there for me
We have a connection, home is where the heart should be...

William Wordsworth and his sister Dorothy

William Wordsworth is viewed today as the most important English Romantic poet. Over the course of his long life, he authored more than five hundred sonnets, and in 1843, was appointed his nation's poet laureate. William's most celebrated masterpiece was his long, auto-biographical poem, *The Prelude: Growth of a Poet's Mind.*

Orphaned as children, he and his younger sister Dorothy—less than eighteen months apart in age—grew to be extremely close. Besides traveling widely as companions, they kept a rural house together for seven years, until William was married in 1802. During this period, they shared an inspirational friendship with the poet Samuel Taylor Coleridge, who lived nearby.

In July 1798, Wordsworth penned *Lines Written a Few Miles Above Tintern Abbey,* among his most beautiful poems. He was twenty-eight at the time. Its stirring lines include these sentiments about Dorothy:

My dear, dear Sister! And this prayer I make,
Knowing that Nature never did betray

The heart that loved her; 'tis her privilege,
Through all the years of this our life, to lead
From joy to joy, for she can so inform
The mind that is within us, so impress
With quietness and beauty, and so feed
With lofty thoughts, that neither evil tongues,
Rash judgments, nor the sneers of selfish men,
Nor greetings where no kindness is, nor all
The dreary intercourse of daily life,
Shall e'er prevail against us, or disturb,
Our cheerful faith that all which we behold
Is full of blessings. Therefore let the moon
Shine on thee in the solitary walk;
And let the misty mountain winds be free
To blow against thee: and in after years,
When these wild ecstasies shall be matured
Into a sober pleasure, when thy mind
Shall be a mansion for all lovely forms,
Thy memory be as a dwelling-place
For all sweet sounds and harmonies; Oh! then,
If solitude, or fear, or pain, or grief
Should by thy portion, with what healing thoughts
Of tender joy wilt thou remember me...

Choosing Paths in Life

·-·-·-·-·-·-·

Sylvia Ashton-Warner and her sister Daphne

Born in Stratford, New Zealand, at the turn of the twentieth century, Sylvia Ashton-Warner was a writer who achieved greatest fame late in life for her work as an educator. Besides writing poetry, she produced several bestselling novels, including *Bell Call, Greenstone, Incense to Idols, Three,* and *Spinster* (the latter was made into the 1961 British film, *Two Loves*). Seeking peace and communication between two radically different cultures, Ashton-Warner adapted traditional British teaching methods to the special needs of Maori children—and thereby gained international stature. With lively, nonfiction books such as *Teacher* and *"Teacher" in America,* she influenced progressive educational methods throughout the 1960s and 1970s.

In Ashton-Warner's autobiography *I Passed This Way,* the writer-educator tenderly recalled a conversation with her dying sister:

"Daph," I asked her decades later when she was staying at my home, very ill, "Why was it that you never did anything with your unique gifts?"

"I had no ambition."

Her eyes were still liquid and her legs like poems. "But," I say, "How could anyone brought up by Mumma have no ambition?"

"It was that summer morning, Sylv. It dated from the time I failed [Math]. I'd failed in front of the family. You, a year younger, had passed. The worst thing, though, was most of them were there to see it."

"But Daph, everyone knew I'd only scraped through by one mark. They all knew your average...even without arithmetic...was higher."

The luminous green of her eyes [turned] reminiscent. "That summer morning, Sylv. That was the first time I'd let down my audience. Not one flick of ambition have I had since."

"But you have more gifts than the lot of us put together. Wherever you are, whomever you're with, the world becomes your stage."

"My family is my stage," [she said] warming up. "I keep my best for my family."

"Others know your best."

"You hear this, Sylv: Only the family matters. Until my last breath. And you take it from me, that last breath itself will be my masterpiece."

Pauline Bonaparte and her brother Napoleon Bonaparte

Napoleon I, also known as Napoleon Bonaparte, crowned himself emperor of France. The leading military figure of his time, he was perhaps history's greatest general. Napoleon was born on the Island of Corsica, in the Mediterranean Sea, the fourth child of Carlo and Leitzia Ramolino Buonaparte (later changed to Bonaparte). The year before, France had bought Corsica from the Italian city-state of Genoa. Napoleon entered a French military school, and quickly rose through army ranks, gaining fame as a brilliant commander during the French Revolutionary period. At the age of twenty-six, he married in May 1796. Later that year, his considerably younger sister, Pauline, also planned to wed. But Napoleon felt she was merely infatuated with editor Louis Freron—a revolutionary nearly twice her age—and strongly advised against the marriage.

In *Pauline, Favorite Sister of Napoleon,* biographer W. N. C. Carlton translated sixteen-year-old Pauline's letter of bitter compliance:

> I have received your letter. It has caused me the deepest pain. I did not expect such a change on your part. You agreed to my union with Freron. You promised to smooth away all the obstacles to it. My heart committed itself to that hope and I looked upon it as the fulfillment of my destiny. I send you his last letter; from it you will see that all the accusations against him are untrue.

As for me, I will choose lifelong unhappiness rather than marry without your consent, and by so doing, draw down upon myself your severe condemnation. You, my dear Napoleon, for whom I have always felt the tenderest affection—if you could see the tears your letter has caused me to shed, you would be touched by them, I am sure. You, from whom I expected happiness, you compel me to renounce the only man I can ever love. Young as I am, I have a steadfast character...I know my duties too well to turn aside from them, but I also know I cannot change according to circumstances.

Adieu. I had to say this to you. Be happy, and in the midst of your victories, think sometimes of the bitterness and tears that fill the life of Pauline Bonaparte.

Confiding About Ambition

Florence Nightingale and her cousin Hilary Carter

As creator of the modern nursing profession, Florence Nightingale ranks among the most important women of the nineteenth century. Celebrated in her own lifetime as the "Lady of the Lamp," she was born in Florence, Italy, where her wealthy parents were temporarily staying and grew up in Derbyshire, Hampshire, and London, where they owned homes. Florence was educated mainly by her father, who taught her Greek, Latin, French, German, Italian, history, philosophy, and mathematics. Throughout her life, she read extensively in many languages. Society life was far less satisfying to her.

At the age of thirty, in 1850, Florence completed training as a nurse, and three years later, she was appointed superintendent of the Institution for the Care of Sick Gentlewomen in London. She made many administrative improvements, but longed for a wider field of action. When the Crimean War broke out in 1854, Florence volunteered at once, and became a national hero for her crusading efforts on behalf of wounded English and French allied soldiers in the Crimean War. In 1856, after much bureaucratic resistance, she was finally appointed general superintendent of the Female Nursing Establishment of the Military Hospitals of the Army.

Later, upon returning home, Florence was instrumental in lobbying for better living conditions among English soldiers stationed in India, and for creating the Nightingale Hospital for Nurses, the first professional institution of its kind in the world. For over fifty years beginning in the mid-1850s, she was renowned internationally for her humanitarian efforts, including the reform of living conditions in England's poorhouses. In 1907, Florence became the first woman ever to receive the Order of Merit from the King of England.

In a revealing letter, most likely penned in May 1843, to her cousin Hilary Carter, Florence at age twenty-three confided her desire for greater independence:

> I am looking forward to next Saturday, if I can go anyhow tacked on to somebody's apron string. How often I wish for grey hairs! They are the greatest possible convenience, and if they could be had before other infirmities, would be as much advantage as Brevet Rank [a special military rank bestowed in wartime].
>
> If anybody wishes to read about the May of life in the little

inkmarks of poets, it's all very well. If they wish to read about it in real life, it is a series of scrapes, of dull bothers and sharp remorse, of useless giving of pain, and hopeless perplexity.

We reckon our young years by their failures and not by their months, and fifty times a day have I remembered, ever since, what an elderly woman once said to me, about the privileges, the joys, the *exemptions* from youth which her age enjoyed.

Confiding About Health Problems

Mary Todd Lincoln and her cousin Elizabeth Todd Grimsley

Mary Todd, from all historical evidence, was adored by Abraham Lincoln. High-spirited, quick-witted, and well-educated, she came from a distinguished Kentucky family, and her Springfield, Illinois, relatives belonged to the social aristocracy of the town. Some of them frowned upon her association with lower-echelon Lincoln, and occasionally, he too had doubts whether he could ever make her happy. But they became engaged, and then married in November 1842.

Mary Todd Lincoln's life was marked by personal tragedy. Besides witnessing her husband's assassination in 1865, she suffered the deaths of three of their four sons; only Robert, the eldest, survived into adulthood. Upon leaving the White House as First Lady, Mary was both a mental and physical wreck. Years of subsequent travel failed to restore her well-being, and she was briefly committed to a private sanitarium in 1875 before eventually going to live with her sister.

During adult life, Mary Todd Lincoln corresponded often with her female cousins. Writing from the White House in September 1861, she sent Elizabeth this sisterly news:

I have been intending writing you for some days. I have been quite sick with *chills* for some days. This is my day of rest, so I am sitting up. But I am beginning to feel very weak. Mr. Lincoln wants me to go north and remain until cold weather.

Where so much is demanded of me, I cannot afford to be delicate. If a different climate will restore my health—if at the close of this week, I am still sick, I expect I will go up to Boston, take quarters at Revere House for two or three weeks, and return here in November…September and October are always considered unhealthy months here, and my racked frame certainly bears evidence to the fact.

The weather is so beautiful, why is it that we cannot feel well? The air feels very much like the early days when I used to have chills in Illinois. Those days have passed, and I know I have no cause to grieve over my lot. If the country was only peaceful, all would be well.

Confiding About Home Life

•••••••

Emily Dickinson and her brother William

Emily Dickinson ranks among America's greatest poets. Known as the "New England mystic," she experimented with innovative poetic rhythms and rhymes. Emily grew up and remained in her hometown of Amherst, Massachusetts, throughout her life. The second of three children, she was close to younger sister Lavina who, like Emily, stayed in the family house and never married, and to her older brother, William Austin, who lived in the house next door after marrying one of Emily's friends. Emily attended Amherst Academy and Mount Holyoke Female Seminary, and began writing verse intensely in the late 1850s. With a spiritually passionate temperament, she was drawn to Ralph Waldo Emerson's transcendentalist outlook.

Emily Dickinson produced over seventeen hundred poems over the ensuing decades, generally involving themes of intimate domestic life and love, nature, and death. After the Civil War, Emily's strength ebbed and she never left the boundaries of her family's estate. Almost all of her extensive body of poetry and letters was published posthumously.

On a Saturday morning in autumn 1851, twenty-year-old Emily in Amherst wrote to her younger brother, Austin, away at college:

> I've been trying to think this morning how many weeks it was since you went away to school—I fail in calculations. Oh, I am so lonely! You had a windy evening going back to Boston, and our fire burned so cheerfully, I wished so many times that the door would open and you would come walking in. Home is a holy thing— nothing of doubt or distrust can enter its blessed portals. I feel it more and more as the great world goes on...Here seems indeed to be a bit of Eden.

Nancy Resedale Mitford and her brother Thomas

Nancy Mitford was one of this century's great British letter writers. A well-known biographer, journalist, and novelist, she was the eldest of Lord and Lady Resedale's seven talented children—writer Jessica Mitford among them. Nancy immortalized her family's life in her first bestseller, *The Pursuit of Love,* and for over a half-century until her death in 1973, was admired for her wit and verve. Her comic novels about English high society and romance included *The Pursuit of Love, Don't Tell Alfred,* and *Love in a Cold Climate*. Nancy's literary friends included Harold Acton, Cyril Connolly, and Evelyn Waugh.

As *Love From Nancy: The Letters of Nancy Mitford,* indicates, she relied upon her brother Thomas as a helpful sounding-board. In this letter of July 1927, twenty-two-year-old Nancy confided her restlessness and ennui at home:

> Depression has the Mitford family in its clutches, the birds never speak save to curse or groan, and the rest of us are overcome with gloom. Really, this house is too hideous for words, and its rather pathetic attempt at aesthetic purity makes it, in my opinion, worse. I mean I would rather it were frankly hideous and Victorian, because then it would at least have atmosphere; whereas, at present, it is like a barn badly converted into a temporary dwelling place and filled with extremely beautiful and quite inappropriate furniture...
>
> I had a terrific row with Mother about staying with [my friend] Nina, and she said, at last, "Go if you like, but I'd rather you didn't," which is rather unsatisfactory, so I said I'd go. Do you think it was very nasty of me? After all, it means a fortnight less here, which is no mean consideration. Also, I think that at age twenty-two, one is old enough to choose one's own friends—don't you?—especially as I'm to pay for it myself.

Confiding About Personal Danger

—————

Dolly Madison and her sister Anna

Dolly Madison was the wife of President James Madison, and a prominent Washington, D.C., hostess. The third child born to Quaker parents in Guilford County, North Carolina, she married Madison in 1794, when he was a well-placed Virginia Congressman. Admired for her personal charm and tact, Dolly entertained on behalf of widower Thomas Jefferson when her husband was his secretary of state. She is probably best known for her brave flight from Washington, D.C., in August 1814, when the British invaded the Capitol during the War of 1812. Dolly saved many important governmental papers and a portrait of George Washington. Just before departing the city, she dispatched a letter to Anna describing what she had done:

> My husband left me yesterday morning to join General Winder. He inquired anxiously whether I had courage or firmness to remain

in the President's house until his return on the morrow or succeeding day, and on my assurance that I had no fear but for him and the success of our army, he left, beseeching me to take care of myself, and of the Cabinet papers, public and private...

I have pressed as many Cabinet papers into trunks as to fill one carriage. Our private property must be sacrificed, as it is impossible to procure wagons for its transportation...

Our kind friend, Mr. Carroll, has come to hasten my departure, and in a very bad humor with me, because I insist on waiting until the large picture of General Washington is secured, and it requires to be unscrewed from the wall. This process was found too tedious for these perilous moments. I have ordered the frame to be broken, and the canvas taken out. It is done! and the precious portrait placed in the hands of two gentlemen of New York for safe keeping.

And now, dear sister, I must leave this house, or the retreating army will make me a prisoner of it by filling up the road I am directed to take. When I shall again write to you, or where I shall be tomorrow, I cannot tell!

Confiding About Political Fears

●—●—●—●—●—●—●

*Mary Wollstonecraft Shelley and her brother-in-law
Alexander Berry*

Certainly best known today for her Gothic horror tale about a scientist who creates a dreadful monster, titled *Frankenstein,* Mary was an English novelist whose other works include *Valpegra, The Fortunes of Perkin Warbeck,* and *The Last Man* (the latter an acclaimed narrative of humanity's future destruction by a plague).

At the age of sixteen, the London-raised Mary met the young poet Percy Shelley in the spring of 1814, and ran off with him to France in July of that same year. The impassioned couple were married in 1816, as Mary came closest as any woman could to Percy's requirement for his life partner: "one who can feel poetry and understand philosophy." After her husband's death in 1822, Mary returned to England to publicize his writings and educate their only surviving child, Percy Florence Shelley.

In March 1848, Mary wrote to her recently widowed brother-in-law Alexander Berry, then living in Australia:

It always gives me pleasure to hear from you. It is pleasant to know that I have a connection so far off who takes interest in my fortunes. Sometimes I have thought that the feeling of solitude with which you felt assailed after losing your dear wife might impel you to revisit this country, and I should have been delighted to give you a cordial welcome... We should be most happy to welcome you under our roof, if the epidemic of revolutions leave us one.

It is terrible to write such words in jest—but these are awful times. The total overthrow of law, the dislocation of the social system in France presents a fearful aspect. In Italy and in Germany, the people aim at political rather than social change, but the French will spare no pains to inculcate their wicked and desolating principles, and to extend the power of their Provisional Government all over Europe... There is no doubt that a French propaganda is spread among all the nations; they are rousing the Irish and even the English Chartists.

I do believe that in England, law and the orderly portion of the community will prevail. God grant it—God preserve us from the tyranny and lawlessness now oppressing France.

Confiding About School

Sylvia Plath and her brother Warren

Born to middle-class parents in Boston, Sylvia Plath ranks among America's most acclaimed post-World War II poets. Plath's autobiographical novel, *The Bell Jar,* is her best-known work. She wrote her first verses at the age of eight, and excelled in school. By the time Plath was accepted to Smith College on a scholarship in 1950, she had already amassed an impressive list of publications. While attending Smith, Plath produced over four hundred poems, but began showing persistent depression. Several years later, she married and had children with the British poet Ted Hughes. At the age of thirty, while the two were struggling financially in London, she took her life.

As presented in her posthumously published volume, *Letters Home,* twenty-year-old Sylvia at Smith College in November 1952 wrote revealingly to her brother, Warren, at home:

My [Princeton] date was the perfect example of [an] absolute sheep, and I thought I could have fun with him. It was all right [with] my brilliance, and he guessed I was not as neutral as I seemed. His confession of his own inadequacies, in an attempt to be serious, was not only pitiably revealing of his lack of thinking and values, but was evidently quite a strain on his mental powers...

No doubt, some of the boys at Princeton are intelligent and nice, but all the ones I saw are spoiled, sheepish socialites, who get drunk all the time and don't have an original or creative impulse. They are all bloodless, like mushrooms inside, I am sure...

My work is overwhelming. Don't know how I have the time to goof off writing letters, but I have two papers due every week from now till Thanksgiving. I'll have to work most of the vacation on my back schoolwork, too. If I live till Christmas, it will be a miracle.

Love you dearly, your galley slave sister, Sivvy.

Confiding About Work Frustration

Marie Sklodowska Curie and her cousin Henrika Michalowska

Marie Curie was a French physicist who became famous for her work on radioactivity. Over the course of her influential life, she received two Nobel Prizes, one in 1903 in physics (with her husband, Pierre, and their colleague Antoine Becquerel), and the other eight years later in chemistry. Marie Curie helped found the Radium Institute in 1914 and served as its first director.

Raised in Warsaw, Marie showed scientific ability at an early age. She came from an intellectual family, and despite the early death of their mother from tuberculosis, two of Marie's siblings became doctors, including her solicitous older sister, Bronia. Before embarking for university study in Paris, where Marie would meet Pierre Curie, she briefly found employment as a governess. Biographer Robert Reid in *Marie Curie* related that at the age of eighteen, in April 1886, Marie was in the midst of her third—and last job governess—when complaining to her cousin Henrika:

> I am living as customary to live in my position. I give my lessons and I read a little, but it isn't easy, for the arrival of new guests constantly upsets the normal employment of my time. Sometimes this irritates me a great deal, since my Andzia is one of those children who profit enthusiastically by every interruption of work, and there is no way of bringing her back to reason afterwards.
>
> Today we had another scene, because she did not want to get up at the usual hour. In the end, I was obliged to take her calmly by the hand and pull her out of bed. I was boiling inside. You can't imagine what such little things do to me; such a piece of nonsense can make me ill for several hours. But I had to get the better of her.
>
> [As for] conversation in company? Gossip and then more gossip. The only subjects of discussion are the neighbors, dances and parties.

Margaret Mitchell and her sister-in-law Frances Marsh

Gone With the Wind, which won the Pulitzer Prize in 1937 and was made two years later into a remarkably popular movie, reflected author Margaret Mitchell's origins and milieu. Born in 1900 to a fifth-generation Georgian, she worked as a reporter for the *Atlanta Journal* before resigning in 1926 to begin writing what would become her only full-length book. Although it took nine years for her to find a publisher and see the novel's release to American readers, *Gone With the Wind* sold a million copies within its first six months.

Vividly set in Civil War and Reconstructionist Georgia, *Gone With the Wind* became an American entertainment phenomenon, offering such memorable characters as beautiful Scarlett O'Hara and dastardly Rhett Butler. Though Mitchell maintained a voluminous correspondence, she never published another novel and tragically died in a car accident at the age of forty-nine.

Biographer Darden Asbury Pryon in *Southern Daughter* recounted that Mitchell was feeling ambivalent and upset about her journalistic work when confiding to her sister-in-law Frances Marsh during mid-spring 1926:

> I am of the opinion that I am through with my job at the *Journal*. I have no business doing it…[My boss] Mr. Perk did me a dirty deal, while I was sick and not being able to walk. I sent John to tell him to shove my job up his—well, the place reserved for such things. Perk is a lousy little beast and I've gotten so tired working for him. However, he sent his wife Medora out to patch things up…but I don't think I'll go back on the magazine, unless the economic pressure becomes too hard to stand…If I stay home long enough, my ankle will get well— instead of going back half-cured because we need the money so damned bad.

When I do get well—if I ever do—I suppose there will be time enough to look for another job. However, John wants me to stop work [at the newspaper] until I'm well, even if we starve, and [my brother] Steve and Father do too. So I guess I will.

Harry Truman and his sister Mary

Harry Truman's presidency was marked by such momentous events as the dropping of the atomic bomb on Japan, the Allies' victory in World War II, the rebuilding of Europe during the emerging Cold War, and the Korean War. During the decades since Truman's administration, historians have come to regard him with increasing respect.

Born and raised in small-town Missouri, Truman was the oldest of three children. Throughout his life, he remained especially close to his sister, Mary, who never married, and in later years, devoted herself to caring for their aged mother. As revealed in *Off the Record, The Private Papers of Harry S. Truman,* even in the thirty-third President's most wearying days, he corresponded with Mary as a valued confidant. In this letter of November 1947, the thirty-third President remarked:

> I've been trying to write you all week, but have been covered up with work and am so tired when night comes, I just fall into bed and go to sleep. Have been trying to get the message ready for the special [Congressional] session and it is a job...[My adversaries] are doing what they can to put me in a hole.

But I've got to face the situation from a national and an international standpoint, and not from a partisan, political one. It is more important to save the world from totalitarianism than to be President another four years. Anyway, a man in his right mind would never want to be President if he knew what it entails...Aside from the impossible administrative burden, he has to take all sorts of abuse from liars and demagogues...Then the family has to suffer too.

They say I'm my daughter's greatest handicap! Isn't that something? Oh, well, take care of yourself, and some day the nightmare will be over, and maybe we all can go back to normal living.

Consoling a Grieving Sister

————

Louisa May Alcott and her sister Anna

Louisa May Alcott is best known for her enduring novel *Little Women*.
Published soon after the end of the U.S. Civil War, it tells the vivid story
of four sisters growing up in a New England town during the
mid-1800s. Its depiction of family life from a woman's perspective made
it an immediate success. The novel gave Alcott lifetime financial
security and a platform for her later activism on social issues from
temperance to women's voting rights.

As an adult, Lousia May Alcott remained especially close to her sister
Anna, and in a letter of December 1870, offered these sympathetic
words on the death of Anna's husband:

> You need not be told what John was to me, or how I mourn for
> him, for no born brother was ever dearer, and each year I loved and
> respected and admired him more and more. His quiet integrity, his

patient spirit, so cheerful and so persistent, his manly love of independence and his brave efforts to earn it for those he loved: how beautiful, simple, and upright his life looks now. Good son, brother, husband, father and friend. I think that record is a noble one for any man, and his thirty-seven years are very precious to those who knew him.

He did more to make us trust and respect men than any one I know, 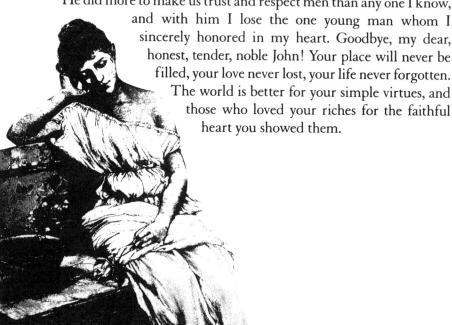 and with him I lose the one young man whom I sincerely honored in my heart. Goodbye, my dear, honest, tender, noble John! Your place will never be filled, your love never lost, your life never forgotten. The world is better for your simple virtues, and those who loved your riches for the faithful heart you showed them.

Discussing Married Life

•••••••

Abigail May Alcott and her brother Samuel

Abigail May Alcott, mother of the novelist Louisa May Alcott, was born in Boston, in 1800, the youngest of twelve children. Biographer Clara Gowing in *The Alcotts as I Knew Them* related that when looking back on her youth, Abigail recalled candidly, "My schooling was much interrupted by ill health, but I danced well and at the dancing school, I had for partners some boys who afterwards became eminent. I did not love study, but books were attractive." At the ate of nineteen, Abigail broadened her education with a private tutor in French, Latin, botany, and history.

She first met her future husband, the social reformer and philosopher Henry Amos Alcott, at her brother the Reverend Samuel May's home. It was apparently love at first sight, for in Abigail's view, she had finally met, at age thirty, "the only being whom I ever loved as companionable." The wedding ceremony at Boston's King Chapel, where Abigail's father was a board member, was performed by Samuel himself. After nearly fifty tumultuous years involving Henry's zealous educational and social reform, the marriage would last until Abigail's death in old age.

In May 1831, several months after Abigail and Amos opened their first school in the Philadelphia area, she sent her brother this warm-hearted letter:

> This is the anniversary of my wedding day, and I devote an hour to you in living over the past and projecting the future. It has been an eventful year—a year of trial, of happiness, of improvement. I can wish no better fate to any sister of the sex than has attended me since my entrance into the conjugal state. Our prospects are good.
>
> I wish you could see our delightful situation. You would not wonder that we went to our last dollar to establish ourselves in this little paradise. Imagination never pictured to me a residence so perfectly to my mind. I wish my friends could see how delightfully I am settled. My father has never married a daughter or seen a son more completely happy than I am. I have cares, and soon they will be arduous ones; but with the mild, constant and affectionate sympathy of my husband, with the increasing health and loveliness of my quiet and bright little Anna, a house whose neatness and order would cope with Federal Court…and a large ground with a beautiful serpentine walk shaded with pines, firs, cedars, apple and plum trees, what can I not do when surrounded by influences like these? What can I leave undone with so many aids?

Amelia Earhart and her sister, Muriel

Amelia Earhart was an American aviator who became the first woman to cross the Atlantic Ocean by air as a passenger, and then to fly across it solo. Born in Atchison, Kansas, she developed an interest in flying while working as a nurse's aide in Canada in 1918, during World War I. By 1922, Amelia at the age of twenty-five had received a pilot's license and begun entering flying contests. Seven years later, she created the "Ninety-Nines," an international organization of women pilots that still exists. Amelia served as its first president from 1930 to 1933. During this period, she married the wealthy publisher George Putnam, but continued her flying career under her maiden name.

As revealed in *Letters From Amelia,* the courageous aviator and her younger sister had a very close relationship. As Muriel's marriage to a dentist in small-town Massachusetts became increasingly strained, Amelia was empathetic and supportive. Writing from Los Angeles in January 1937, just a few months before vanishing without a trace in an apparent plane crash near Howland Island in the central Pacific Ocean, Amelia pointedly advised:

> You've taken entirely too much on the chin for your own good or that of any man who holds the purse strings. I sometimes feel that adult human beings owe as much to themselves as to others, for by asserting individual rights, the baser natures of those who have them

are held in check. That is often very hard to do. One hesitates to bring on a quarrel when it can be avoided by giving in. But perhaps one definite assertion will prevent the slow accumulation of a sense of superiority in a person who really should not claim superiority. Given a little power over another, little natures swell to hideous proportions. It's hopeless to watch a character change of this kind in one you have cared for: a few [fights] might have been less suffering in the long run…[but] what's done is done…

You had better plan to come out here for the summer. Or before, if you have to. Something can be worked out. It is hard to give up the school just when it is beginning to pay, but human crises have a way of happening at inconvenient times.

Edith Jones Wharton and her sister Minnie

As one of America's leading novelists writing in the early 1900s, Edith Wharton is best known for works including *Ethan Frome, Twilight Sleep,* and her Pulitzer Prize-winning *The Age of Innocence.* Such novels depicted the upper-class society into which Wharton was born and raised. In 1885, she married the Boston banker Edward Wharton, and a few years later, resumed the literary career she had begun tentatively as a teenager. Her major literary model was Henry James, whom she knew, and her work reveals James' concern for artistic form and ethical issues.

In 1907, Edith Wharton moved to France, subsequently visiting the United States only rarely, especially after divorcing her husband. Two years prior to that event, in September 1911, Wharton, while vacationing at a health spa in Salsomaggiore, Italy, related to her sister Minnie:

Just after I wrote you the other day, your dear kind letter came back from the Mount, and I must tell you before you sail how it touched me. The first few weeks (after you and Henry were with us) were about as bad as they could be, and finally, I struck, packed my trunk, and departed for Newport, saying I've had enough of it. After two weeks of prayers and entreaties (in which Billy Wharton took an energetic part), I said I would "give another trial," and this time Teddy seemed at last to realize that he must pull himself together—and did so.

In short, this episode seems to have done more than all the doctors put together toward restoring his nervous equilibrium. From that time till I sailed, he was perfectly good-tempered, reasonable and "nice," and I want everyone to know that, as far as I can judge, he is now quite well again.

Encouraging Education

●━●━●━●━●━●

Abigail Smith Adams and her sister Mary

Abigail Adams has a unique place in American history. An influential patriot during the Revolutionary War, she was married to one president (John Adams) and mother to a second (John Quincy Adams). Born in Weymouth, Massachusetts, to a family of Congregational ministers, Abigail lacked formal education, as did other women of her time. However her curiosity sparked her keen intelligence, and she read widely.

Long separations kept Abigail from her beloved husband, John, while he served as a delegate to the Continental Congress, an envoy abroad, and an elected officer under the newly crafted Constitution. The two were married for more than fifty years and raised five children. Respected for speaking forthrightly on many issues, Abigail often relied upon her more demure sister Mary as a sounding-board. In a typical letter, dated February 1787, Abigail offered this advice on education:

Knowledge would teach our sex candor, and those who aim at the attainment of it—in order to render themselves more amiable and useful in the world—would derive a double advantage from it, for in proportion as the mind is informed, the countenance would be improved and the face ennobled as the heart is elevated: for wisdom, says Solomon, makes the face to shine.

Sometimes, as the following letter dated July 1789 reveals, Abigail also relied upon Mary for tactfully eliciting guidance from "near and intimate friends":

It is to desire them to watch over my conduct and if at any time they perceive any alteration in me with respect to them—arising as they may suppose from my situation in Life—I beg they would with the utmost freedom acquaint me with it. I do not feel within myself the least disposition of the kind, but I know mankind prone to deceive them, and some are disposed to misconstrue the conduct of those whom they conceive placed above them.

Pat Ryan Nixon and her brother William Ryan

Early life was hard for Thelma Catherine Ryan, who acquired her nickname, Pat, within hours of her birth in Nevada. Her Irish father, William, a miner, dubbed her "St. Patrick's babe in the morn" when he arrived home before dawn on March 16, 1912. Soon the family moved to

California and settled on a small truck farm near Los Angeles. After the death of her mother, Kate, thirteen-year-old Pat had to assume all the household duties for William and two older brothers. At eighteen, she lost her father after nursing him through months of illness.

Left on her own, Pat was determined to continue her education. Holding a series of part-time jobs on campus, as a salesclerk in a fashionable department store and as an extra in the movies, she graduated cum laude from the University of Southern California in 1937. She accepted a position as a schoolteacher in Whittier and there met Richard Nixon, who had returned home from Duke University Law School to establish a practice. They became acquainted in a little theater group when cast in the same play and were married in June 1940. Throughout her husband's all-consuming political career, she was tirelessly supportive while raising two daughters, Tricia and Julie, and once remarked, "It takes heart to be in political life."

In *Pat Nixon, the Untold Story,* Julie Nixon Eisenhower related that her mother was "on contract" as an actress for Paramount Studios when writing her brother Bill this letter in February 1933. He was feeling lonely and downcast at Fullerton College, so Pat offered these encouraging sentiments:

> I'd be awfully mad if you play too much and don't get good grades. There's no excuse, because you have the brains, and you must develop the willpower to concentrate and strive to win. Maybe we

could go somewhere to school together: that would be swell, and we'd practically be in the same grade.

The world is just what we make it, so let's make ours a grand one. Too, it's fun to work and then enjoy the fruits of the success.

Expressing Faith and Spiritual Contentment

George Eliot (Mary Ann Evans) and her cousin Sara Hennel

George Eliot was the pen name of Mary Ann Evans, one of England's great nineteenth-century writers. *Silas Marner* and *Middlemarch* are her most famous novels—reflections on the middle-class, a rural childhood, and youth. Though writing seriously about moral and social problems of her time, Eliot created memorable characters as well.

In October 1847, twenty-eight-year-old Eliot was vacationing on the Isle of Wight—and yet a dozen years away from publishing her first novel, *Adam Bede,* when she wrote to her devoted cousin Sarah:

> I do long for you to see Alum Bay. Fancy a very high precipice, the strata upheaved perpendicularly in rainbow-like streaks of the brightest maize, violet, pink, blue, red, brown, and brilliant white, worn by the weather into fantastic fretwork, the deep blue sky above and the glorious sea below. It seems an enchanted land, where the

earth is of more delicate, refined materials than this dingy planet of ours is wrought of.

I find one very spiritual good attendant on a quiet meditative journey among fresh scenes. I seem to have removed to a distance from myself when I am away from the petty circumstances that make up my ordinary environment. I can take myself up by the ears and inspect myself like any other queer monster on a small scale...

I think "Live and teach" should be a proverb as well as "Live and learn." We must teach either for good or evil; and if we use our inward light as the Quakers tell us, always taking care to feed and trim it well, our teaching in the end must be for good. We are growing old together—are we not? I think I am growing happier, too.

Alice James and her brother William

Alice James, sister to the celebrated novelist Henry James and the Harvard philosopher-psychologist William James, struggled with poor health throughout her life. Highly intelligent, sensitive, and educated abroad, Alice could never marshal the willful creativity that enabled her two older brothers to achieve such notable success. For decades, she fruitlessly sought treatment in private sanatoriums for chronic fatigue, depression, and other ailments. In 1889, Alice was already a semi-invalid living near her brother Henry in London when she began keeping a diary—recently acclaimed by literary scholars—to record her wide-ranging daily observations.

In July 1891, less than a year before Alice's death at the age of forty-four, she offered William her own, strong spiritual outlook:

It is the most supremely interesting moment in life, the only one in fact when living seems life, and I count it the greatest good fortune to have these few months—so full of interest and instruction—in the knowledge of my approaching death. It is as simple in one's own person as any fact of nature, the fall of a leaf or the blooming of a rose, and I have a delicious consciousness, ever present, of wide spaces close at hand, and whisperings of release in the air...

When I am gone, pray don't think of me as simply a creature who might have been something else, had neurotic science been born. Notwithstanding the poverty of my outward experience, I have always had a significance for myself, and every chance to stumble along my straight and narrow little path, and to worship at the feet of my Deity, and what more can a human soul ask for?

This year has been one of the happiest I have ever known, surrounded by such affection and devotion...Give much love to all the household, great and small.

Expressing Love and Gratitude

••••••

Mary Baker Eddy and her brother George

Founder of the faith known as Christian Science, Mary Baker was born on a New Hampshire farm. She had limited schooling because of illness, but studied at home and began writing both prose and poetry while still a child. During a difficult period marked by her first husband's death at an early age and her own worsening health problems, Mary found healing solace in the Bible. She authored her influential "textbook" *Science and Health* in 1875, a work which her numerous followers came to regard as divinely inspired. Organizing the First Church of Christ four years later in Boston, Mary Baker Eddy (taking the name of her third husband, Asa Eddy) later founded the weekly *Christian Science Sentinel* and the *Christian Science Monitor,* a well-respected daily newspaper.

In September 1835, fourteen-year-old Mary was quite frail when writing to her older brother George. At the time, he was idealistically teaching textile weaving to Connecticut prison inmates:

> If solitude will make one's thoughts flow on uninterrupted, I think I shall have plenty of them this afternoon as Father, Mother, and Martha (which makes up the family) has gone to attend the funeral of J. L. Cravis, and I am left alone to review past events...Still, as you informed us in your letter, you enjoyed contentment and health at which I do most sincerely rejoice...
>
> There is one thing I have learned from experience to prize perhaps more than ever—and that, dear brother, is the friendly advice and council you have given me, and the lively interest you have manifested in my welfare. Now, when I sit down to my lonely meal, as I have no brother Sullivan [who left home] to encourage me as formerly, I must extend the thought of benevolence farther than selfishness would permit and only add that my health at present is improving slowly, and I hope by dieting and being careful to sometimes regain it...
>
> Write every opportunity, excuse all mistakes as this is the second letter I ever wrote, and accept the well wishes of your affectionate sister.

Katherine Beauchamp Mansfield and her brother Leslie

Katherine Mansfield, a British author, wrote symbolic short stories about everyday human experiences and feelings. Many of these reflect her affluent childhood in Wellington, New Zealand, often involving her brother, Leslie, and herself as chief characters. Mansfield's well-received stories were published in collections, in chronological order, entitled *A German Pension, Prelude, Bliss,* and *The Garden Party.* Her posthumously published *Journal* in 1927 offered a fascinating picture of her creative mind and her writing's development.

Residing in London, Mansfield began college as a precocious teenager. An unhappy marriage at a young age was followed by an equally unsuccessful affair and a miscarriage. Her wealthy parents then sent her to Baveria to convalesce; these experiences helped form the basis of her first book. She later married the essayist John Middleton Murray and became a member of a literary circle that included Virginia Woolf and D. H. Lawrence. Mansfield was plagued by health problems during adulthood and died of tuberculosis at the age of thirty-four.

In August 1915 Katherine Mansfield wrote these tender words in an Oxford Street, London reading-and-writing room to Leslie. Unknown to each, this would prove their final message for one another; five weeks later, he was killed instantly by a grenade explosion while fighting in France.

I have an odd moment to spare, and I'll use it in sending you a line. Ever since last Sunday, you are close in my thoughts. It meant a tremendous lot, seeing you and being with you again, and I was so frightfully proud of you. You know that, but I like saying it. But the worst of it is I want always to be far *more* with you, and for a long enough time for us to get over the "preliminaries" and live together a while.

Do you know a day when your heart feels much too big? Today if I see a flag or a little child or an old beggar my heart expands and I would cry for joy. Very absurd. I'm twenty-six, you know. This is not a letter. It is only my arms around you for a quick minute.

Anna "Bamie" Roosevelt and her sister-in-law
Edith Carrow Roosevelt

Bamie Roosevelt was three years older than her famous brother Theodore, who became the twenty-sixth president of the United States. From their childhood days onward in New York City and Sagamore Hill, Long Island, the two were extremely close, and throughout Theodore's adult life, she remained among his closest confidants. In 1884, when on the same day his first wife, Alice, died tragically in childbirth and his mother died from typhoid, Theodore became despondent and left New York State politics to run two cattle ranches in the Dakota Territory. With the rough-and-tumble lifestyle needed for such work, he found his mental outlook improving. During several trips back home, Theodore visited a childhood friend, Edith Carrow, and the two became secretly engaged.

Buoyed with renewed interest in life, Theodore decided to re-enter politics, and ran for mayor of New York City. As cited by David McCullough in his book *Mornings on Horseback,* an enthusiastic Bamie Roosevelt in October 1886 kept her future sister-in-law informed of the candidate's progress:

> It is such happiness to see [Theodore] at his very best once more; ever since he has been out of politics in any active form, it has been a real heart sorrow to me, for while he always made more of his life than any other man I knew, still with his strong nature it was a permanent source of poignant regret that even at this early age, he should lose these years without the possibility of doing his best and most telling work…
>
> This is the first time since [Assembly] days that he has enough work to keep him exerting all his powers. Theodore is the only person who had the power except Father, who possessed it in a different way; of making me almost worship him and now it is such a desperate feeling to realize that in all this excitement, I cannot help him in the least except that he knows how interested I am.
>
> I would never say or write this except to you, but it is very restful to feel how you care for him and how happy he is in his devotion to you. I go back tomorrow [to Sagamore Hill], and wish you were to be there also as you were the last.

Imparting the Secrets of Success

●—●—●—●—●—●

Katharine Meyer Graham and her sister Bis Meyer

The daughter of a Wall Street tycoon and a Washington power broker, Katharine Graham was raised by one of the most politically influential families of the twentieth century. From the day her father bought the *Washington Post* in 1933, her life has been marked, and sometimes scarred, by the ups and downs of politics in Washington, D.C. After her husband, Phil Graham's, suicide in 1963, Katharine was suddenly faced with publishing the *Post* herself. Despite an awkward start, she went on to publish the Pentagon Papers and allow reporters Woodward and Bernstein to crack open the Watergate scandal that led to President Nixon's resignation.

Today Katharine Graham is a bestselling author, preeminent Capitol Hill hostess, and—according to some Washington insiders—among the most powerful women in the world. As recounted in Katharine

Graham's memoir, *Personal History,* she grew up close to her mother and siblings. In a letter dated November 1937, twenty-year-old Katharine received this intriguing advice from her older sister Bis:

> One of the hardest problems for all of us is…the difficulty arising from the fact that from earliest childhood we have all, through what is said and unsaid in the family circle, had the feeling that we were born to do big things! There was no question but that whatever it was, we had to be best at it. Mother even used to say that, remember? "I don't care what any of you kids do—even if one of you should want to be an actress—just so you're a hell of a good actress!"
>
> We have all felt a compulsion to be terrific! And that is a dangerous thing.
>
> It is awfully hard for us really to give our best to something low, small, unimportant. We have lived so long at the top in every respect that it is hard to make ourselves really at home, with roots, at the bottom of the mountain. And that is the only way we will ever grow, if any of us do, to be able to climb under our own power.

Improving Writing Ability

———

Caroline Darwin and her brother Charles

Charles Darwin was an English naturalist who became famous for his theories on evolution. Published in 1859, his *On the Origin of the Species by Means of Natural Selection* is among the world's most influential scientific works. Charles' mother died when he was only eight years old and, because his father never remarried, his older sister, Caroline, became a surrogate mother. She took interest and pleasure in her gifted brother's developing scientific career, and the two corresponded regularly after he began traveling as a naturalist-explorer.

Darwin, age twenty-four, was aboard the English expedition ship H.M.S. *Beagle* when Caroline penned him this useful and encouraging literary advice:

I have been reading with the greatest interest your journal and found it very entertaining and interesting. Your writing at the time gives such reality to your descriptions and brings every little incident before one with a force that no after-account could do. I am very doubtful whether it is not pert in me to criticize, using merely my own judgment, for no one else in the family has yet to read this last part—but I will say just what I think—I mean as to your style.

I thought in the first part (of your last journal) that you had, probably from reading so much of Humboldt, got his phraseology and occasionally made use of the kind of flowery French expressions which he uses, instead of your own simple, straightforward and far more agreeable style. I have no doubt you have without perceiving it go to embody your ideas in his poetical language, and from his being a foreigner, it does not sound unnatural in him.

Remember, this criticism only applies to parts of your journal, the greatest part I liked exceedingly and could find no fault, and all of it I had the greatest pleasure in reading.

Ellen Tucker Emerson and her brother Edward Emerson

Ellen Tucker Emerson was the oldest child of America's leading nineteenth-century philosopher, Ralph Waldo Emerson, and his second wife, Lydia. Attending several of the country's most innovative schools of her day, Ellen became knowledgeable in French, German, Greek, and Latin with smatterings of both Italian and Spanish. She accompanied her father on two of his lecture trips to Europe, and was a keen observer of the many famous visitors who came to Concord, Massachusetts, to meet him.

Over the decades, Ellen Emerson was a prolific correspondent and diarist, and came to know and record her impressions of such luminaries as Henry David Thoreau, Henry Alcott and his daughter Louisa May, Nathaniel Hawthorne, and William James. Most of Ellen's time and energy in adult life went into housekeeping, staying close with her relatives, caring for her parents in their old age, and helping James Elliot Cabe edit her father's unpublished writings for posterity.

In April 1872, Ellen was at home in Concord when offering this intriguing advice to twenty-eight-year-old Edward:

> Tell always of the present. We want to know how you do, what you are about, whom you see, how it seems to be all alone. You used to be an Emerson and knew that the trifles of every day are interesting, but seem lately to have imbibed the common belief that writing about one's self is egotistical and that only [unusual] events are worth chronicling. Please remember too that persons are more interesting than places, and you can make us acquainted with the persons about you.
>
> I'm so afraid of hurting and discouraging you, and seeming ungrateful for all your delightful letters. But being an Emerson, that can't keep me from telling [you] what I think on both sides. Now, your last week's letter to me was model, all about persons and the present.

Nurturing a Sick Brother

————•••••••————

Agnes Crane and her brother Stephen

Stephen Crane was a prolific American novelist, short-story writer, poet, and journalist. Although he died of tuberculosis in his late twenties, Crane produced a vast body of newspaper articles, more than one hundred stories including "The Open Boat" and "The Blue Hotel," literary sketches, two volumes of poetry, and six novels. Published in 1895, his most famous novel is *The Red Badge of Courage,* a story set during the Civil War. It portrayed a young Union soldier who undergoes a transformation from cowardice to heroism amidst the noisy confusion and "crimson roar" of the battlefield.

Crane pioneered in psychological realism, often exploring the thoughts of fictional characters facing death. In *Stephen Crane: A Biography,* scholar R. Stallman recounted the writer's childhood, as the youngest of fourteen children, raised in rural Port Jervis, New Jersey:

Stephen was nearly seven now, but he had not yet been to school.

A delicate child, he had been nursed by his sister Agnes during the previous year, and perhaps the question of his health was one of the reasons for the family's settling in Port Jervis with its mountain air in nearby Harwood.

It was Agnes who saw after Stephen's education in his early years. She combed his long curls, which were not shorn until he was eight, and taught him whatever he learned about nature, lore, science and literature. Agnes said she wanted to be a "Christian lady" first of all and then to write. Very proud of her brother's first writings, she remained his closest companion until her death when she was only twenty-eight.

Ada Lawrence and her brother D. H. Lawrence

D. H. Lawrence was a highly influential English novelist. He was born in the coal-mining town of Eastwood, in 1885, and grew up with two sisters. Despite chronic poor health, Lawrence produced many short stories, poetry, and novels exploring love, sex and intimacy such as *Women in Love, The Plumed Serpent, Sons and Lovers,* and his most famous, *Lady Chatterly's Lover.* He traveled widely in an effort to overcome his tubercular condition, to which he finally succumbed at the age of forty-five. Lawrence kept journals based on his trips to Australia, Italy, and Mexico, and these supplied the background for many of his works.

In November 1911, while Lawrence's older sister, Ada, was nursing him back from a nearly fatal bout of pneumonia, she sent his lover, Louise, this letter:

> Doctor says Bert is no worse—tomorrow or next day is the crisis—and please God, all may be well; the disease of the left lung has not spread further. Last night, he had a morphine injection and therefore had a fairly good night. He wanders a great deal [in his

speech], but when sensible, he talks of you often. Don't write him, my dear, until he's passed the crisis, for he hasn't been able to read anything for over a week. I've told [only] little bits of his letters and even that has excited him...

We are all fighting hard for him. Keep a brave heart for his sake, and try not to worry, or when he sees you, he will know. As soon as ever he can bear, I shall send for you.

Grandma Moses (Anna Mary Robertson) and her brother Fred

"If I didn't start painting, I would have raised chickens" quipped Anna Mary Robertson, a crusty, feisty, upstate New York farmwoman and grandmother who gained fame in the mid-twentieth century for her primitive artistry. After raising ten children and working hard at a variety of jobs, Anna devoted herself full-time to art in the 1930s, when she began exhibiting her work—mostly of placid rural life—in county fairs. Discovered in the window of a Hoosick Falls, New York, drugstore by a Manhattan art collector in 1938, Anna's paintings were soon placed on exhibit in the Museum of Modern Art, and eventually featured in leading art galleries and publications. Anna became a celebrity over the next two decades, and her hundredth birthday in 1960 was virtually a day of national celebration. Anna died the following year. On her headstone, the inscription reads: "Her primitive paintings captured the spirit and preserved the scene of a vanishing countryside."

In *Grandma Moses, My Life's Story,* edited by Otto Kalir, the famous artist recalled:

Brother Fred was a baby then, about three months old, and he was hungry, and cried and kept crying. We couldn't stop him. Mother was quite sick with the measles. Father said, "He's hungry," so I went to the pantry and fixed him a coffee cup full of bread and milk, and I used a good deal of the top milk, with sugar on it. I set it on the edge of the stove to keep it warm, then took Fred and wrapped a cloth under his chin and commenced feeding him that bread and milk. I fed all of it to him. He went off to sleep. He had never had anything but breast milk up to that time.

Fred slept all night and way into the next morning. When father came in about 11 o'clock, I asked him to look at the baby, which he did, and he said, "Fred is all right." He was still asleep at 3 o'clock in the afternoon, when mother said, "I wish you would bring me the baby, he hadn't ought to sleep like this."

I went to the cradle and picked Fred up, but I didn't dare uncover his face...for I feared I should not have fed him bread and milk and that he was dead. As mother lifted the veil from his face, she said, "Oh my goodness!" and then I knew he was gone! I turned to look, and his face was as red as red could be. He was all broken out in measles!

But Fred has lived to be an old man, and is in his seventies now.

Offering Character Advice

———————

Susan B. Anthony and her sister Mary

Susan B. Anthony is honored today as among America's most important feminist advocates. As a pioneering crusader for women's right-to-vote and a president of the National American Woman Suffrage Movement, Anthony's work helped pave the way for the Nineteenth Amendment to the U.S. Constitution in 1920. Born in 1820, she grew up in a home dominated by her Quaker father's zealous abolitionism. A precocious child, Anthony learned to read and write at the age of three. After attending several schools in upstate New York and then Philadelphia, Anthony became a school teacher near her family home in the Rochester area. Founding the Woman's State Temperance Society of New York, Anthony soon turned her attention to women's rights, and beginning in the 1850s, worked alongside her friends Elizabeth Cady Stanton and Amelia Bloom. Anthony was also prominent in abolitionist efforts prior to the Civil War, and for more than fifty years until her death in 1906, her name was associated with political activism and courage.

Kathleen Barry related in *Susan B. Anthony: A Biography of a Singular Feminist* that soon after finishing her Quaker school as a teenager, Susan had a vivid dream in which her younger sister, Mary, behaved in a sulking, uncooperative manner. Susan told Mary the disturbing dream, and later felt obliged to add this advice:

> Rest assured, Dear Sister, that we all regard you equally with the rest, but that particular trait in your character we so dislike, and sincerely hope you may be enabled to command strength to overpower it, and thus secure your own happiness, as well as those around you. Do not indulge anger toward anyone, for that will also make you unhappy. Suffer yourself to think about serious things and Death, for that will strengthen you in doing well.

Maria Edgeworth and her brother Henry

Born in mid-eighteenth-century Oxfordshire, England, Maria Edgeworth achieved fame for her children's stories and vivid novels of Irish life. At the age of fifteen, she relocated with her family to the Dublin area, where as oldest daughter, Maria helped her father manager the family estate. In this way, she acquired her knowledge of rural economy and of the Irish peasantry that was to be the backbone of her novels.

Encouraged by her father, Maria began writing in the common sitting room, where the other twenty-one children in the family provided material and a lively audience for her stories. She published them in 1796 as *The Parent's Assistant,* and her first novel, *Castle Rackrent,* four years later. Her next novel, *Belinda,* was especially admired by Jane Austen.

Edgeworth enjoyed a wide literary and scientific acquaintanceship, and was especially friendly with novelist Sir Walter Scott. In her later years, Edgeworth was active managing the family estate and provided humanitarian aid for the hard-pressed Irish peasantry.

In March 1805, Maria was already a well-received writer when she penned these supportive words to her younger brother Henry at Edinburgh:

> I think you are quite right in all your Union and anti-Union battle. It gives me the most sincere pleasure to see your letters to father just as if you were talking to a favorite friend of your own age, and with that manly simplicity characteristic of your mind and manner from the time you were able to speak. There is something in this perfect openness and in the courage of daring to be always yourself, which attaches more than I can express, more than all the [clever] arts and graces that were ever practiced.

Golda Mabovitch Meir and her sister Shenya Mabovitch

Golda Meir served as prime minister of Israel from 1969 to 1974 and held several key cabinet posts during her long career. Born in the Ukraine, she emigrated as a child with her family to Milwaukee, Wisconsin, in 1906 and later taught public school there. She relocated to the Holy Land in the early 1920s and became steadily more active in political affairs while raising two children in a difficult marriage.

In her autobiography, *My Life,* Golda Meir recalled her hard youthful years in the Ukraine:

> Still, not everything could have been so fearful. I was a child, and like all children, I played and sang and made up stories to tell the baby. With Shenya's help, I learned to read and write and even do a little arithmetic, although I didn't start school in Pinsk, as I should have. "A golden child," they called you," my mother said. "Always busy with something." But what I was really busy doing in Pinsk, I suppose, was learning about life—again, chiefly from Shenya.
>
> Shenya was fourteen when Father left for the United States: a remarkable, intense, intelligent girl who became and who remained, one of the great influences of my life, perhaps the greatest, apart from the man I married. By any standard, she was an unusual person, and for me, she was a shining example, my dearest friend and my mentor. Even late in life, when we were both grown women—grandmothers,

[actually], Shenya was the one person whose praise and approval, when I won them, which was not easy, meant most to me.

Shenya, in fact, is part of the story of my life. She died [three years ago], but I think of her constantly, and her children and grand-children are as dear to me as my own.

In the winter of 1920, Golda was actively planning to settle in the Holy Land and become strongly involved in Zionist politics. Living in Chicago at the time, Shenya wrote frequently to Golda, and warned that her younger sister was getting too involved in matters of public, rather than private, concern:

As far as personal happiness is concerned, grasp it, Goldie, and hold it tight. The only thing I heartily wish you is that you should not try to be what you *ought* to be, but what you *are*. If everybody would only be what they are, we would have a much finer world.

Providing Career Encouragement

●━━━━━━●

Virginia Louise Meredith and her brother Burgess

Burgess Meredith was one of our century's most accomplished actors and directors. Born in Cleveland, Ohio, and educated at Amherst College in Massachusetts, Meredith's film and theater career spanned seven decades. His stage debut came in 1933 in New York, and his screen debut, at age twenty-six, was in the 1936 drama, *Winterset,* recreating a role he had played on Broadway. Meredith would go on to appear in nearly seventy movies, mostly in supporting roles. He starred in the 1939 film version of John Steinbeck's *Of Mice and Men* and as the Penguin character in the 1966 *Batman* movie and subsequent *Batman* television series, approaching the role with his usual thoroughness.

"I waddled like a penguin, which seemed rather obvious to do," Meredith recalled. "The touch I liked was that peculiar penguinlike quack I used in my lines." Probably, Meredith achieved greatest fame for his portrayal of the feisty boxing manager in the highly popular *Rocky* movie series. Yet, such success seemed almost miraculous to Meredith in later life. In his memoir, *So Far, So Good,* the famous actor reminisced:

>...I am still warmed by the memories of my older sister, Virginia Louise Meredith. I loved her, and that love still shadows my reminiscences. She raised me, fed me, encouraged me as best as she could.
>
>[My sister and her husband] lived at one time on Central Park West...and I was singing as a boy soprano in the great choir at the Cathedral of St. John the Divine nearby on 110th Street and Amsterdam Avenue.
>
>I came from Lakewood, Ohio, a suburb of Cleveland. There I was more or less pushed into the career of singing, in spite of my asthma...and I was entered into a nationwide audition for the Paulist Choristers Boy Choir of New York...(I won the Cleveland audition, and was scheduled to participate the following spring in New York City). About this time, my sister and brother-in-law moved there and began to have second thoughts about my attending a Roman Catholic choir school!
>
>[So] before we reported to the [Catholic] church, my sister arranged another audition for me, at the Protestant Cathedral of St. John the Divine—the largest church in America...The leader of the choir in those days was Dr. Miles Farrow, who explained that if he

liked my voice, I could become one of forty boys who made up the soprano section in that vast cathedral.

Dr. Farrow and his colleagues were intrigued to meet the prize-winner of the rival Paulist choir: the lad who would turn down [the church's] offer. They auditioned me, then accepted me...

So at the ripe old age of ten, I joined the Cathedral of St. John the Divine choir—I hope my mother or sister properly notified the good Father Finn—and my life changed. I came into a different culture, a new way of life, and new friends...

Providing Emotional Support

••••••

Sarah Muir and her brother John

John Muir was one of the greatest explorers and naturalists in American history. An eloquent writer who extolled nature's grandeur, he inspired the early conservation movement in this country. Scotland-born Muir also possessed strong faith and viewed his calling in almost religious terms. Among his many accomplishments, in 1890 he effectively influenced Congress to pass the Yosemite National Park Act, establishing both Yosemite and Sequoia national parks.

Throughout Muir's colorful life, he enjoyed tramping around the globe, including North America, Europe, Africa, and even the Arctic. With a restless temperament, he could never reside in one place for very long. In February 1875, thirty-seven-year-old Muir was staying in Oakland, California, when he penned this letter to his older sister Sarah:

I spent my holidays on the Yuba and Feather Rivers exploring. I have, of course, worked hard and enjoyed hard: ascending mountains, crossing canyons, rambling ceaselessly over hill and dale, plain and lava bed.

I thought of you, all gathered with little ones enjoying the sweet and simple pleasures that belong to your lives and loves. I have not yet in all my wanderings found a single person so free as myself. Yet, I am bound to my studies and the laws of my life. At times, I feel as if driven with whips, and ridden upon. When in the woods, I sit at times for hours watching birds or squirrels or looking down into the faces of flowers, and suffer no feeling of haste. Yet, I am swept onward in a general current that bears on irresistibly. When, therefore, I shall be allowed to float homeward, I *dinna, dinna ken,* but I hope [soon].

The world, as well as the mountains, is good to me, and my studies flow on in a wider and wider current by the incoming of many a noble tributary. When I visit you, you will all have to submit to numerous lectures. Remember me as ever lovingly your brother, John.

Mabel Wolfe and her brother Thomas

Though he lived only thirty-eight years, Thomas Wolfe achieved fame for his autobiographical novels, including *Look Homeward, Angel; Of*

Time and the River; and the posthumously published masterpiece *You Can't Go Home Again.* With startling yet tender poetic imagery, Wolfe's writing was often disorganized but carried great emotional impact.

Wolfe grew up in small-town Asheville, North Carolina, before the first World War. It was not a milieu that favored literary precocity, but Wolfe's family saw his talent early on and encouraged it zealously. Wolfe was close emotionally with his sister, Mabel, and in the weeks prior to the publication of his first autobiographical novel, *Look Homeward, Angel* in 1929, he was consumed with worry about how Asheville's populace—many of whom knew his family personally— would react to it. In *Look Homeward: A Life of Thomas Wolfe,* his biographer David Donald related:

> Wolfe spent a good deal of time with his sister Mabel, who now lived in an expensive house on Kimberly Avenue, looking across the golf course to the Grove Park Inn. She gave a party in his honor and invited the best that Asheville could muster in the way of writers and educators. But Wolfe got an inkling that Ralph Wheaton's [his brother-in-law] future with the National Cash Register Company was uncertain, and he was sensitive to the constant, nagging friction between his sister and her demanding mother-in-law...
>
> After a week in Asheville, Wolfe was still extremely worried about how local townspeople would react to *Look Homeward, Angel.* Mabel, the person with whom he had discussed the book most

extensively, assured Thomas that, "No more than ten people in Asheville would read it."

But she became both confused and a little frightened when her brother insisted, while waiting for his train back to New York City: "Now, when I come next time, Mabel, I'll probably be wearing a beard or whiskers. I'll have to come incognito…I have written a few things about [folks] here in Asheville that I'm afraid some of them aren't going to like."

Providing Protection

—•—•—•—•—

Clara Barton and her brother Stephen

Renowned as the founder and first president of the American Red Cross, Clara Barton—dubbed the "angel of the battlefield"—was an influential figure throughout the second half of the nineteenth century. After serving as a Massachusetts school teacher for eighteen years, Barton settled in Washington, D.C., and became a clerk in the U.S. Patent Office. At the outbreak of the Civil War, she organized an agency to obtain and distribute supplies for the relief of wounded soldiers. In 1865, at the request of an impressed President Lincoln, she set up a bureau of information to aid in the search for those missing-in-action.

In the ensuing thirty-five years, Barton achieved international acclaim in both the United States and Europe for her work with the Red Cross on behalf of wounded soldiers and civilians suffering from natural calamities such as floods, famines, pestilence, and earthquakes.

She also wrote several books including *History of the Red Cross* and *The Red Cross in Peace and War*.

In March 1861, Barton was already actively working for the Northern Union cause in Washington, D.C., when she urgently penned this advice to her younger brother, Stephen:

> Our Government has for its objective the restoration of the Union as it *was,* and will do so, unless the resistance of the South prove so obstinate and prolonged that the abolition or overthrow of slavery follow as a consequence...
>
> And this brings me to the point of my subject: here comes my request, my prayer, supplication, entreaty, command—call it what you will, only heed it, at once—COME HOME. Not home to Massachusetts, but home to my home—I want you in Washington. I could cover pages, fill volumes, in telling you all the anxiety that has been felt for you, all the hours of anxious solicitude that I have known in the last ten months, wondering where you were, or if you were at all, and planning ways of getting to you, or getting you to me, but never until now has any safe or suitable method presented itself.

After instructing Stephen how to escape via Union naval transport and thereby reach Annapolis, Clara ended with a flourish:

> I am a plain Northern Union woman, honest in my feelings and counsels, desiring only the good of all, disguising nothing, covering

nothing and so far, my opinions are entitled to respect and will be received with confidence. If you will do this as I suggest, and come to me at once in Washington, you need have no fears of remaining idle…Washington has never had so many people and so much business as now.

Marie Cuomo and her brother Mario

As New York State's governor for twelve years until 1994, Mario Cuomo often referred to his working-class origins with pride and eloquence. His mother, Immaculata, and father, Andrea, were Neopolitan immigrants who came to the United States in the late 1920s.

Lacking formal schooling, Andrea Cuomo cleaned sewers for several years before saving enough money to open a grocery store in a multiethnic New York City neighborhood. "It was open twenty-four hours a day, and by the time I was born in 1932," his famous son later recalled, "my father was making a living from sandwiches he made in the early morning for the construction crews and quick midnight snacks he prepared for the night shift across the street…Almost everything he did, he did for his children." Of course, Immaculata was ceaselessly busy helping to manage the store and the Cuomo household.

In *Mario Cuomo,* biographer Robert McElvaine humorously recounted:

Immaculata Cuomo appointed her daughter, Marie, to be the "little mother" for her brothers. She ordered them around and threatened them with reports to their parents. "You scrub the stairs the right way! Otherwise, I'll tell Momma." It was always: "I'll tell Momma and Poppa," Frank Cuomo remembers. These arrangements did not invariably work out for the best.

On one occasion when Mario was about four or five, his mother had to work in the [family grocery] store and left Marie in charge of the toddler: "You take care of Mario. Walk him. Hold him by the hand." But as they passed the Golden Cup bakery down the block, a delivery truck roared up an inclined alley at them. In her fright, Marie let go of her little brother's hand and he fell. The truck went right over him. Thinking her brother had been killed, Marie ran away screaming. She went into hiding at Rufus King Mansion park.

When Marie finally came back, she went in tears to a neighbor across the street whom they called Tia (Aunt) Paulina...She told the woman her sad tale and asked her to go and break the news to her parents.

In fact, the truck wheels had completely missed Mario and Tia Paulina found him sitting at home having cookies and milk and "being treated like a king."

He didn't have a scratch on him. "Typical Mario luck," the former governor reminisced.

Jane Fonda and her brother Peter

The award-winning actress of such films as *Julia, The China Syndrome, The Morning After,* and *On Golden Pond,* seems to have been destined at an early age to an uncommon and influential life in the limelight. The daughter of screen star Henry Fonda and socialite Frances Seymour Brokaw, Jane Fonda at the age of twenty-three made her movie debut with *Tall Story* in 1960. Her appearance in several risque films including *Barberella* by then-husband Roger Vadim was followed by what was to become Jane's most controversial period: advocating anti-establishment causes and seeking to end the U.S. war effort in Vietnam. Her political involvement continued with fellow activist and husband Tom Hayden in the 1970s and early 1980s. Later, Jane Fonda catalyzed the aerobic exercise craze with the publication of *Jane Fonda's Workout Book* and hugely successful video series. In 1991, she married broadcasting mogul Ted Turner.

Born in New York City, the young Jane and her brother Peter were close, suffering through their parents' bitter divorce and their mother's subsequent suicide. As adults, the two Fonda siblings shared a passionate concern for social justice and protection of the environment. In *Citizen Jane,* biographer Christopher Anderson related:

> En route from his home in Aspen, Colorado, to his ranch in Livingstone, Montana, Peter had a brief stopover in Denver. At the

airport terminal, he came across a sign taped to a phone booth. Posted by the pro-nuclear Fusion Energy Foundation, it read: "FEED JANE FONDA TO THE WHALES." Jane's brother whipped out his pocket knife, tore the sign to shreds—and was promptly arrested for destroying private property.

"She's my sister, and in my neck of the woods," Peter declared, "you don't get away with saying anything bad about someone's sister, mother, or grandmother." When two witnesses failed to appear in court, the charges were dropped.

Miriam and her brother Moses

Moses and Aaron have been revered for millennia as leaders of the Israelite exodus from slavery in Egypt to eventual freedom in the Holy Land. But according to the Hebrew Bible and folklore, their sister, Miriam, was a masterful prophet in her own right, as well as an artful dancer and musician who played the tambourine. *The Book of Exodus* (2:1–11) clearly tells how Miriam was instrumental in Moses' survival as an infant and subsequent entry into Egypt's royal family:

> Now a man from the house of Levi went and took to wife a daughter of Levi. The woman conceived and bore a son; and when she saw that he was a goodly child, she hid him three months. And when she could hide him no longer, she took for him a basket made

of balrushes, and daubed it with bitumen and pitch; and she put the child in it and placed it among the reeds at the river's brink.

And his sister stood at a distance, to know what would be done to him. Now the daughter of Pharaoh came down to bathe at the river, and her maidens walked beside the river; she saw the basket among the reeds and sent her maid to fetch it.

When she opened it, she saw a child; and lo, the babe was crying. She took pity on him and said, "This is one of the Hebrews' children."

Then his sister said to Pharaoh's daughter, "Shall I go and call you a nurse from the Hebrew women to nurse the child for you?" And Pharaoh's daughter said to her, "Go."

So the girl went and called the child's mother. And Pharaoh's daughter said to her, "Take this child away, and nurse him for me, and I will give you your wages."

So the woman took the child and nursed him. And the child grew, and she brought him to Pharaoh's daughter, and he became her son, and she named him Moses, for she said, "Because I drew him out of the water."

According to legend, this good deed of Miriam as a child for their father and mother (Amram and Jochebed), and for Moses' "foster mother" Thermut, was so magnificent to God that it gave the Israelites a special blessing as they wandered in the desert wilderness.

Phoebe Anne (Annie) Oakley and her brother John

Born Phoebe Anne Moses in 1860, in Darke County, Ohio, Annie Oakley achieved a worldwide appeal that few in her era possessed. Dubbed by Chief Sitting Bull as "Little Sure Shot," Annie stood only five feet tall and weighed one hundred pounds, but her shooting accuracy became legendary in her own lifetime. For over sixteen years, she starred in *Buffalo Bill's Wild West* show; when Annie out-shot the great exhibition marksman, Frank Butler, he fell in love with her, and they were happy the rest of their lives. Once, at the invitation of Kaiser Wilhelm II of Germany, Annie captured international publicity by shooting the ashes off a cigarette he was holding in his mouth. A prominent advocate of women's rights during the first World War, Oakley offered to raise a regiment of women sharpshooters for home service, but the U.S. Army turned her down.

While still a child, Annie became a professional gameshunter and sharpshooter. Her small income enabled the impoverished, rural Moses family to survive financially, and finally pay off their home's mortgage.

In *The Life and Legacy of Annie Oakley,* biographer Glenda Riley recounted:

> One day, Annie's younger brother John had a dangerous scrape with an infuriated wild boar. The snorting, bristling animal, his

mouth dripping white froth, pinned John under the house with no avenue of escape from being mauled.

With quick resourcefulness, Annie helped dig a sizable hole and pulled little John through to save his life. "The angry brute charged," she humorously reminisced, "But it was too late. His nose came through the hole, but we hit it with a heavy spade, and in an hour the wild boar slipped out to the road, uttering threats as he went."

Benjamin Spock and his sister Hiddy

Benjamin Spock was America's most influential pediatrician through much of the twentieth century. When *Baby and Child Care* was published in 1941, it was an immediate success through sheer word-of-mouth, and became a veritable bible for millions of parents. Eventually translated into dozens of languages, *Baby and Child Care* began with these encouraging words: "Trust yourself. You know more than you think you do."

The eldest of six children, Spock was born in turn-of-the-century New England in an era of gas lamps and horse drawn carriages. As a youngster, he was exceedingly shy and timid; only after winning a gold medal with the Yale crew in the 1924 Olympics, did he begin to grow confident in his own abilities. After medical school, Spock became the first physician ever to train in both pediatrics and psychoanalysis. Later, when seeking to build up his struggling practice in Depression-era New

York City, Spock was invited to write a parenting manual. His editor's advice: "It doesn't have to be very good, we're only going to charge a quarter."

In *Benjamin Spock, an American Life,* biographer Thomas Maier recounted the famous pediatrician's early years:

> Hiddy, only a year-and-a-half younger, was his constant playmate. They'd go roller-skating along a sidewalk or fly a kite in a local park. Hiddy was a bouncy, tomboyish little girl with a cherubic face. Benny admired her gumption. "Even as a small child, she was a very independent, spunky girl," Spock recalls. "At that time, I had become a rather wistful, somewhat timid child who would never think of standing up to my Mother."
>
> Hiddy, who kept her straight brown hair flopped over to one side and usually tied back with a white bow or clip, cheerfully helped her big brother, in his quest to become a man. To learn how to smoke cigars, for instance, she and Benny gathered leaves fallen from a large rhododendron and rolled them with corn silk. After a few puffs, they coughed until they turned all shades of purple.

On the way to school, the Spock children walked past the neighborhood bully's house.

> Each morning, as this slightly older boy caught sight of Benny, he'd come out and shout all sorts of threats. "Ben was scared to death

of him," remembers Hiddy. "I used to challenge this boy: *Don't you dare do anything to my brother.*" And I became his protector. If anybody was going to do anything to Ben, I would just ball my fists up and go at them like this." Almost a century later, Hiddy could still put up her dukes, jabbing and poking, just as she did during those headlong encounters in New Haven.

Elie Wiesel and his sister Tsipouka

Elie Wiesel is probably the world's most influential Holocaust survivor and spokesperson. Born into a religious Jewish-Romanian family in the village of Sighet, Wiesel was sixteen years old when deported, along with his entire family and all his Jewish neighbors, to the Auschwitz concentration camp. His parents and younger sister Tsipouka were killed, but young Wiesel was forced into slave labor at Buchenwald, another German deathcamp. After World War II ended, he settled in France, where he studied at the Sorbonne and became a journalist. In 1956, he relocated to the United States and acquired citizenship.

Wiesel's first novel, *Night,* chronicled his experiences at the hands of the Nazis, and was followed by works including *Dawn, The Town Beyond the Wall, A Beggar in Jerusalem,* and many others. In 1985, Wiesel was awarded the U.S. Congressional Gold Medal of Achievement, and the following year, he won the Nobel Peace Prize.

Traveling frequently around the globe as a lecturer, Wiesel holds a professorship at Boston University. In his memoir, *All Rivers Run to the Sea,* Wiesel wrote adoringly—and for the first time—about his sister Tsipouka:

> I loved to watch her bending over a book. Serious and intent with her golden hair, she was as beautiful as an angel. I would hold my breath so as not to disturb her. What I felt for her I will never feel for anyone else.

Wiesel vividly recalled the night his baby sister was born:

> At one point my grandmother told me to knock on [our rabbi's] window…"Ask him to intercede for your mother in heaven."
> Naturally, I obeyed. The *Rebbe* wasn't sleeping. His lighted window was open, and he seemed to be waiting for me. "Come in," he said, and then, "Let's go downstairs to the Beit Hamidrash [House of Study and Prayer]. So we went, and there he opened the Holy Ark, stood before the sacred scrolls, and invited me to recite a psalm with him.
> "It is impossible that a child like you and an old man like me would not be heard in heaven." Verse upon verse, we recited the appropriate psalm. "Another," said the *Rebbe,* frowning. I obeyed. After the third psalm he fell silent and I went home. Through the closed door I could hear my grandmother begging my mother: "Don't hold back! Cry! Shout! You have to shout when it hurts, and I know it hurts."

I went back to the *Rebbe*. "It's not working," I told him. "My mother won't shout."

"Very well," he said. "Let's open the prayer book." He found something that spoke to my mother's condition and recited a verse which I repeated after him. Suddenly we heard a piercing cry from across the street. The *Rebbe* leaned over to kiss the book. "You see?" he said. "Our people have just been enriched by a new child. May God bless it."

My little sister was a blessing.

Natalie (Natasha Gurdin) Wood and her sister Lana

Born to Russian immigrants in San Francisco, Natalie Wood debuted in 1943, at the age of four, in the film *Happy Land*. Even in her late teens, Natalie was regularly cast to play the part of a young girl; most notably in *Miracle on 34th Street,* still shown often on television each year during the Christmas holiday season. Educated on the lots of both Fox and Paramount Studios, by the time Natalie was eight years old, she was earning a thousand dollars weekly as the family breadwinner. Nominated for her first Academy Award in 1955, for her part in *Rebel Without a Cause,* she became the queen of fan magazines (sharing that role with Elizabeth Taylor) and one of the world's most popular actresses. Natalie was nominated in the 1960s for two more Academy

Awards, for her role in *Splendor in the Grass* and *Love With the Proper Stranger*.

At the age of forty-three, Natalie tragically drowned, leaving behind a legacy of over forty-five movies. In *Natalie, a Memoir by Her Sister,* Lana Wood, who likewise developed an acting career, vividly recalled:

> I was in awe of my sister…A smile or a caress from Natalie, or a talk with her—these were the highlights of my life. She had many smiles for me, and was always ready to talk, to answer all my questions. Not even my own mother was that patient…
>
> Natalie was my surrogate parent, the person I knew would protect me from any danger. One night, Mother got us up in matching red dresses, and she and Pop took us out for dinner. We were driving across a bridge when Natalie saw a car strike a child. Natalie gasped in horror, and when I looked up to see what was happening, Natalie pulled me into her lap and hid my face in her arms. I struggled a bit as my curiosity got the best of me, but Natalie's embrace was as complete as it was tense, and I remained in her arms, my face buried on her chest. She held me hard, her body rigid. I knew I was safe.

Providing Reminiscences About Growing Up

●━━━━━━●

Izabela Walesa and her brother Lech

Lech Walesa has been an acclaimed reformer and political leader of Poland for the past generation. Born in the village of Popowo in 1943, he was the son of a carpenter and received only elementary schooling followed by vocational training. As a young man, Walesa went to work as an electrician at the Lenin Shipyard in Gdansk, and in 1970, he became involved in protests against higher, government-imposed food prices. In the ensuing rioting, many workers were gunned down by troops. A decade later, during more anti-government activity, Walesa helped to organize scattered protest into the Solidarity labor movement, and became its head.

When the Polish government suspended Solidarity and imposed martial law in 1981, Walesa was arrested and detained for nearly a year. He won the Nobel Peace Prize in 1983 and, pressing vigorously for economic and political reforms, was elected president of Poland in 1990, serving in this post for five years. Today, some credit Walesa and his Solidarity movement for spearheading the ending of Soviet-Communist rule over Eastern Europe.

In his well-received autobiography, *A Way of Hope,* Walesa effectively personalized his nation's dark, tormented history through much of the twentieth century. Poland's former president opened his book evocatively with these words:

> I will begin with my family history. I have my [older] sister Izabela to thank for jogging my memory and more. The records and memoirs she has collected reflect the experiences of a simple Polish family; the people, that house, and those fields I know so well, with men and women bearing the same name as mine.
>
> It's the wild mallows my sister—my only sister—still sees when she looks through her bedroom window. During those summers, they were the first thing you caught sight of on waking; nature's way of salvaging a hint of poetry from the surrounding grayness. These mallows continued to play their part in my reminiscences...creating in our young eyes an illusion of abundance and profusion, of vigorous life.

Rejoicing in Nostalgia

━━━━━━━

E. B. White and his sister Marion

The creator of such enduring children's works as *Charlotte's Web, Stuart Little,* and *The Trumpet of the Swan,* E.B. White grew up in New York City during the first decade of the twentieth century. After receiving his degree from Cornell University in 1921, he began his literary career as a newspaper journalist and then worked in advertising. Publishing his first article for *The New Yorker* in 1925, White joined the staff as an associate editor two years later. For many decades, he was chief contributor to its regular column known as "Notes and Comments."

White was renowned as a stylist whose prose works were the hallmark of *The New Yorker's* witty, intelligent, and well-crafted pieces. Relocating with his wife, Katharine, to rural Maine in the mid-1950s, White in later life received many literary honors including the Presidential Medal of Freedom in 1963, the Laura Ingalls Wilder Award bestowed by the American Library Association in 1970 for "a lasting contribution to children's literature," and a special Pulitzer Prize citation in 1978 for the body of his work.

In April 1952, White was fifty-three years old when he offered his older sister, Marion, these warm sentiments:

> Congratulations to you and Arthur on your fiftieth anniversary! I guess I am a little closer to the right date than when I tried to greet you on your birthday a year ago. I seem to remember that I missed that one by about a month.
>
> How does it feel to be a golden bride? I'd like to drive out some day this week, maybe Friday, and pay you a little call in honor of the occasion. I'll call up in advance to make sure you're home.
>
> If you were married in 1902, I must have been almost three years old; and unless I am much mistaken, your wedding is just about my earliest memory. I distinctly recall our parlor being roped off to form an aisle. And you must have been the gal who walked it. How the years do roll, and wouldn't it be nice if we could slow them up a bit!

Katherine Beauchamp Mansfield and her sister Jeanne Beauchamp

As noted earlier in this book, Katherine Mansfield was a celebrated British short-story writer. Raised in an affluent New Zealand family in the late nineteenth century, she suffered from poor health throughout her short adult life. While "taking the cure" for tuberculosis at scenic Chalet des Sapins in Valais, Switzerland, an ailing Katherine in September 1921 penned these words to her sister Jeanne:

Your handkerchief is such a gay one it looks as though it had dropped off the hanky tree. Thank you for it, darling. I remember the birthday when you bit me! It was the same one when I got a doll's pram, and in a rage, I let it go hurtling by itself down the grassy slope outside the conservatory. Father was *awfully* angry, and said no one was to speak to me. And Aunt Belle had brought from Sydney [Australia] a new recipe for icing. It was tried on my cake, and wasn't a great success because it was too brittle. I can see and feel its smoothness now.

Ah, Jeanne, anyone who says to me, "Do you remember?" simply has my heart. I remember everything, and perhaps the great joy of Life to me is in playing just that game, going back with someone into the past…

Come off with me for a whole day, will you? And let's just remember.

Relating Exciting News

———————

Dorothy Dow and her sister Frances

Dorothy Dow as one of Eleanor Roosevelt's most trusted secretaries. For virtually the entire, twelve-year tenure of FDR's presidential administration spanning the Depression and World War II, she had personal access to the First Lady and her inner circle of family, friends, and advisors. Born in small-town Wisconsin, Dorothy came to Washington, D.C., in 1930 as a young woman eager for adventure. Three years later, she found herself plunged into the heart of Washington's political life as a secretary in the White House Social Bureau serving the new First Lady. As this letter (edited by Ruth McClure in *Eleanor Roosevelt: An Eager Spirit*) dated Easter Sunday, 1934, makes clear to her sister Fran back in Wisconsin, Dorothy was enthusiastic about her duties:

> Today is "Easter Egg Rolling Day" at the White House, and what a jam there is! We have attempted to get some work out, but it is

rather useless. There are mobs of people screaming right by our windows, the band is playing, children screaming and crying because they are lost—and it is just hopeless. I decided for the last half-hour I was going to write personal letters and even give up the pretense of working...

Mrs. Roosevelt has been out three times today to greet people. She is the best person I ever saw. We were outside when she came down the last time, and she isn't satisfied just to stay in a sheltered place and wave at the people. She pushes her way right into the crowd and shakes hands with all she can. It is terribly hot out today, but that doesn't seem to make a bit of difference to her. She is certainly the most socially-minded person I have ever seen. I am sure that if I told you what her program has been for today, you would be exhausted just thinking about it.

We are plenty busy here at work. Have thousands of letters that are not yet answered, but we keep plugging along and have a very kind and considerate boss who doesn't worry, so we aren't pushed.

Relating Motherly Joy

————

Fanny Burney and her brother James

One of England's first popular women writers, Fanny Burney became famous in her own lifetime as a novelist. Today she is best known for her first novel, *Evelina, or a Young Woman's Entrance Into the World,* first appearing anonymously in 1778. Describing a virtuous and intelligent, but innocent, female character in London society, *Evelina* was an immediate success. As a result, Burney became acquainted with the great writer Samuel Johnson and his prominent literary circle. She later wrote *Cecilia, or Memoirs of an Heiress,* a novel dealing with a young woman's financial and marital problems. Burney is also known for her vivid seventy-year diary, published posthumously, depicting English social affairs during her lifetime.

In June 1795, Fanny was forty-three years old when celebrating her recent motherhood in this letter to her brother James:

The little *Idol of the World* is this day half a year old, and more brilliant in beauty, more waggish in wit, and more numerous in noises than ever. In short, if I had not given him this label before, I could this day have chosen no other. I am sure my beloved sister will find every consolation for her lost home and habitation under your roof that affection and true kindness can give.

Remembering a Departed Brother

Eleanor Roosevelt and her brother Hall

Eleanor Roosevelt was respected not merely as the wife of President Franklin D. Roosevelt during America's darkest period, but also as a distinguished public figure in her own right. She was probably the most active First Lady in U.S. history, as well as serving as a delegate to the newly formed United Nations after World War II and chairperson of its Human Rights Commission.

A role model for women as a lecturer, writer, and social activist, Eleanor was also strongly involved with family matters. Her brother, Hall, died of sudden illness in late 1941, two weeks after the demise of Eleanor's mother-in-law. In *The Autobiography of Eleanor Roosevelt,* America's popular former First Lady later recalled:

> The loss of a brother is always a sad breaking of a family tie, but in the case of my brother, it was like losing a child. He had come to live with us when we were first married and from then on Franklin and I

had been his closest family; whatever happened to him, in spite of his great desire for independence, he always came to us...

As I look back on the life of this man whom I dearly loved, who never reached the heights he was capable of reaching, I cannot help having a great sense of sorrow for him, knowing that he must often have felt deeply frustrated and disappointed by his own failure to use the wonderful gifts that were his.

Sorry in itself and the loss of someone whom you love is hard to bear, but when sorry is mixed with regret and a consciousness of waste, there is added a touch of bitterness which is even more difficult to carry, day in and day out. I think it was in an attempt to numb this feeling that I worked so hard at the Office of Civilian Defense that year.

Sophie Thoreau and her brother Henry David

Henry David Thoreau was an American writer who in works like *Walden, The Maine Woods,* and *A Week on the Concord and Merrimack Rivers* has become an icon for his celebration of nature and simple living, and his opposition to anti-human institutions of his era, especially slavery. Born and raised in Concord, Massachusetts, Thoreau became close with the older, far more successful, writer-philosopher Ralph Waldo Emerson, whose transcendentalist spiritual outlook he heartily shared. Spurned by the one woman he loved, Thoreau remained a lonely bachelor. A prolific writer, he crafted beautiful essays—about nature and the human soul—which gave him a devoted following, but brought meager financial reward.

In May 1862, seven weeks after Henry David's death from tuberculosis at the age of forty-four, his sister Sophie penned these words to one of his many correspondents:

> My brother Henry's illness commenced a year ago last December. During seventeen months never a murmur escaped him. I wish that I could describe the wonderful simplicity and child-like trust with which he accepted every experience. As he said, he never met with a disappointment in his life, because he "always arranged so as to avoid it." He learned when he was a very little boy that he must die, and of course, he was not disappointed when his time came. Indeed, we cannot feel that he has died, but rather has been *translated* [into the afterlife].
>
> I never knew anyone who set so great a value on Time as did my brother. He continued to busy himself all through his sickness, and during the last few months of his life, he edited many papers for the press, and he did not cease to call for his manuscripts till the last day of his life.
>
> While we suffer an irreparable loss in the departure of my most gifted brother, still we are comforted and cheered by the memory of his pure and virtuous soul…He was the happiest of mortals, and this world was a paradise for him. "Where there is knowledge, where there is virtue, where there is beauty, where there is progress, there is now his home."

Remembering a Departed Sister

———————

Mary Hunter Austin and her sister Jennie

Mary Austin wrote more than thirty books of lyrical fiction, naturalist description, and autobiography including *Cactus Thorn, The Basket Woman,* and *Earth Horizon.* In 1903, her first book, *The Land of Little Rain,* was published to immediate acclaim. It chronicled her experience homesteading the Mojave Desert. Spending much of her adult life in California and New Mexico, Austin devoted considerable attention to Native American and Hispanic culture, and to environmental issues affecting the region. Her literary acquaintances included Jack London, Willa Cather, Lincoln Steffens, and the desert photographer Ansel Adams.

Growing up semi-impoverished in rural Illinois, Mary Austin loved reading, and by the age of seven, decided to become a writer. She began experimenting with putting words together, but received scant parental encouragement. In *Mary Austin, Song of a Maverick,* biographer Esther Stineman observed:

> Only Jennie, gentle and loving, always understood how Mary felt. With this little sister, who seemed almost an extension of herself, she could share her most sensitive experiences. Together they wandered in the woods and meadows, where Mary sat for hours observing the pattern of a leaf or flower, the design of the bark or branches of a tree, the evocative image of how a shadow fell.
>
> The presence of Jennie was never a distraction. Upon the lovely, delicate child, she centered the full force of a basically affectionate nature otherwise often repressed.

In *I—Mary,* biographer Augusta Fink additionally related:

> "[Her father's] death, though not unexpected, left a void in Mary's life that was deepened by Jennie's death of diphtheria in December of the same year. The guilt that Mary experienced after her sister died profoundly affected her life and work. Her mother had not summoned the doctor for Jennie because Mary had initially shown symptoms of a sore throat and then recovered. Moreover, Mary knew that Jennie was a favorite child and always believed that her mother held her responsible for Jennie's death.

> More than fifty years later, Mary Austin in her autobiography

reflected: "The loss of her is never cold in me, tears start freshly at the mere mention of her name. She was the only one who ever unselflessly loved me. And I would not have it otherwise. She is the only one who stays."

Margaret Fuller and her sister Julia

Margaret Fuller was an important American journalist and social reformer of the mid-nineteenth century. Born in Cambridgeport near Boston, she became a teacher affiliated with the transcendentalist movement headed by Ralph Waldo Emerson; through his influence, she assumed editorship of *The Dial* in 1840. Soon after, Fuller became literary critic on Horace Greeley's newspaper, *The New York Tribune*. In this position, she encouraged new American writers and crusaded for social reforms including women's rights. Her books included *Papers on Literature and Art* and *Woman in the Nineteenth Century*. As America's first women foreign correspondent, Fuller was well-received in English and French literary circles. Together with her husband and their infant son, Fuller died at the age of forty in a shipwreck off Fire Island, New York.

In an anthology of Margaret Fuller's writings, *The Woman and the Myth*, edited by Bell Gale Chevigny, the famous nineteenth-century writer poignantly recalled:

My earliest recollection is of a death—the death of a sister, two years younger than myself. Probably there is a sense of childish endearments, such as belong to this tie, mingled with that of loss, of wonder, and mystery: but these last are prominent in memory. I remember coming home and meeting our nursery-maid, her face streaming with tears. That strange sight of tears made an indelible impression. I realize how little I was of stature, in that I looked up to this weeping face; and it was often seemed since, that full-grown for the life of this earth, I have looked up just so, at times of threatening, of doubt, and distress, and that just so has some being of the next higher order of existences looked down, aware of a law unknown to me, and tenderly commiserating the pain I must endure in emerging from my ignorance.

I did not then, nor do I now, find any beauty in [funeral] ceremonies. What had they to do with the sweet playful child? Her life and death were alike beautiful, but all this sad parade was not. Thus my first experience of life was one of death. She who would have been the companion of my life was severed from me, and I was left alone. This has made a vast difference in my lot. Her character, if that fair face promised right, would have been soft, graceful and lively; it would have tempered mine to a gentler and more gradual course.

Sharing a Séance for a Departed Father

Barbra Streisand and her brother Shelley

As a movie actress, director and producer, singer and stage performer, Barbra Streisand is unequalled today. Her film *The Prince of Tides* was the first motion picture nominated for Best Director by the Directors Guild of America and received seven Academy Award Nominations. Recipient of an honorary degree from Brandeis University in 1995, Barbra is a rare honoree: the only artist to earn Cable Ace, Emmy, Golden Globe, Grammy, Oscar, Peabody, and Tony Awards. With over forty gold, twenty-five platinum, and thirteen multi-platinum albums, she continues to be the biggest-selling female recording artist ever.

Raised with her older brother, Shelley, in Brooklyn, New York, by her young widowed mother, Barbra was an honor student at Erasmus Hall High School and then plunged into a performing career without family assistance or encouragement. She soon developed a following in

New York City's nightclubs. In 1962, Barbra's debut album with Columbia Records proved highly successful, and two years later, she gained national attention with her Broadway debut in *I Can Get it for You Wholesale,* followed by *Funny Girl.* Many film and stage roles followed, including *What's Up Doc?, The Way We Were, For Pete's Sake,* and *A Star Is Born.* Despite such career success, by the late 1970s Barbra was ambitious for greater artistic accomplishment and became interested, despite industry skepticism, in bringing Isaac B. Singer's Yiddish story *Yentl* onto the big screen and playing its major character, Anshel. In *Barbra Streisand: A Biography,* Anne Edwards evocatively related:

> On a trip to New York in the fall of 1979, she accompanied Shelley to their father's grave in a Jewish cemetery in Queens... Shelley took a photograph of [Barbra] standing beside it. When it was developed the following day, she was surprised to observe that the name ANSHEL was carved on the tombstone of the grave adjoining that of Manny Streisand.
>
> "I couldn't believe it," Barbra later recalled. "That's a very unusual name...And right there next to my father's grave was a man named Anshel, who was Yentl's dead brother, whose name she takes when she distinguishes herself as a boy. To me, it was a sign.., from my father that I should make this movie."

Soon after the siblings went to a medium, they sat with their hands on a tabletop.

"And then it began. The table began to spell out letters with its legs. Pounding away. Bang, bang, bang! Very fast, counting our letters. Spelling M-A-N-N-Y, my father's name, and then B-A-R-B-R-A.

"I got so frightened I ran away, because I could feel the presence of my father in that room. I ran into the bathroom and locked the door. When finally I came out, the medium asked: 'What message do you have?' and the table spelled out S-O-R-R-Y. Then the medium asked, 'What else do you want to tell her?' And it spelled S-I-N-G and P-R-O-U-D. It sounds crazy, but I knew it was my father who was telling me to be brave, to have the courage of my convictions to sing proud. And for that word S-O-R-R-Y to come out... I mean, God! It was his answer to all that deep anger I had felt about his dying...And I thought, I have to stand up for what I believe in. I can't be frightened anymore...I should make that movie *Yentl.*"

Sharing Childhood Affection

●━━●━●━●━●━●

Barbara Pierce Bush and her brother Scott Pierce

Among the most popular First Ladies to live in the modern White House is Barbara Bush. Raised in affluent Rye township just north of New York City, sixteen-year-old Barbara met George Bush at a 1941 Christmas week dance in nearby Greenwich, Connecticut; the two became engaged the following year. A graduate of Smith College, Barbara married George during World War II's final year. During the ensuing decades, she raised a family of four sons and aided her husband's diplomatic and political career.

In the bestselling *A Memoir,* the former First Lady recalled:

> [My brother] Scotty was born when I was five. He broke his arm at age two, and the family discovered that he had a "cyst." That started some five years of operations. The surgeons took bone chips from his hip and both shins and implanted them in the arm. He

spent forever in the hospital after the operations, and then months in bed at home with one cast, or sometimes two casts, on. I really don't know what he had but it was an enormous worry for our parents, not only emotionally but financially...

I remember Mother reading the *Wizard of Oz* books to him, and eventually he learned to read them himself. One of the presents he got was multicolored stripes; we made paper chains and hung them from the four posters on his bed. I seem to remember armies of soldiers all over his bedspread, too. I'm sure he complained, but I don't remember it at all. I only remember him as being a great pleasure. Finally, the last operation succeeded, and Scott also went on to become a great athlete. If the four of us [children] voted on "Who do you feel the closest to, who's the kindest, etc.," I suspect we all would say Scotty.

Frederick Douglass and his sisters Eliza and Sarah

A former escaped slave, Frederick Douglass—originally named Frederick Augustus Washington Bailey—was the first black citizen to hold high rank in the U.S. government and one of the most eminent human rights leaders of the nineteenth century. Born on a Maryland plantation in 1817, to a slave mother he never knew and a white father, Douglass was secretly taught to read (in violation of state law) by a slave owner's wife in Baltimore. He later fled to New York City and

Massachusetts, where he changed his name to Douglass to avoid slave-hunters. In 1841, at a Nantucket anti-slavery rally, Douglass was invited to describe his feelings and experiences under slavery. His spontaneous remarks proved so moving that he was unexpectedly catapulted into a new career as an agent for the Massachusetts Anti-Slavery Society. From then on, despite heckling and mockery, insult, and violent personal attack, Douglass never flagged in his devotion to the abolitionist cause. He traveled to Great Britain and Ireland, and for two years, lectured there widely to expand abolitionist sentiment. Eventually, he bought freedom for himself and his entire family.

During the Civil War, Douglass was a consultant to President Lincoln, and in the Reconstructionist era, he fought for full rights for freed slaves and supported the women's rights movement as well. In his final years, Douglass held several civil service positions in Washington, D.C., and served as U.S. minister and consul general to Haiti.

In his famous autobiography called *Narrative of the Life of Frederick Douglass as an American Slave,* he recalled the day when first re-united with his siblings:

Grandmother pointed out my brother Perry, my sister Sarah, and my sister Eliza, who stood in the group. I had never seen my brother nor my sisters before; and though I had sometimes heard of them, and felt a curious interest in them, I really did not understand what they were to me, or I to them. We were brothers and sisters, but what of that? Why should they be attached to me or I to them? Brothers and sisters we were by blood, but *slavery* had made us strangers...The domestic hearth, with its holy lessons and precious endearments, is abolished in the case of a slave-mother and her children. "Little children, love one another" are words seldom heard in slave cabin.

Letty Konigsberg and her brother Woody Allen

Award-winning comedian, actor, and prolific director Woody Allen has occupied a unique status in American film for over thirty years. After graduating from Brooklyn's Midwood High School in 1953, he began his career as a paid jokester and then as an award-winning comic television writer. Subsequently, Allen (née Konigsberg) became a standup comedian, and debuted in the 1965 film as scriptwriter-actor in *What's New, Pussycat?* As director, his most acclaimed movies include *Annie Hall, Manhattan, Interiors, Zelig, Crimes and Misdemeanors, Hannah and Her Sisters,* and *Bullets Over Broadway.*

In *Woody Allen,* biographer Eric Lax highlights the famous comedian's close, lifelong bond with his sister, for in Allen's own words, "Letty and I are just one of those things that are luck. I liked her from the moment I met her." Lax commented: "Virtually from the time she could walk, he took Letty nearly everywhere with him and they remain close today. His interest in her was total and, he says, without jealousy."

As Letty humorously reminisced:

The big factor in my upbringing is that I had him. We were very close.

Here you have a boy who for eight years was an only child. For good or bad, everything focused on him. Into the picture comes this baby who's a girl on top of it—and easier, more compliant, whatever...But you can deal with it one of two ways. You can hate this person, in which case you kind of alienate yourself because obviously these people wanted another child if after eight years they've had one. Or it's a question of "Don't fight 'em, join 'em," and give yourself that special position. "This is my sister. I *love* my sister. This is fantastic!" And then everyone says, "What a brother he is! Look at that! He is terrific! Did you ever see such a relationship? He is just wonderful! He is just great to her!" Thereby avoiding all the negative things that would have happened. There was never any conflict between us. My parents never had to say to him, "Look at how you're treating her." He never received negative attention for how he was with me; he was constantly praised. We developed a very good relationship that didn't have to wait as with many siblings until they're older and can sort out all the garbage. So for me, it was an enormous benefit...that he never had. It took the edge off of the domination by my parents.

Mia Farrow and her brother Michael

Mia Farrow is the daughter of the director John Farrow and the actress Maureen O'Sullivan. At the age of fourteen, Mia debuted with several small film roles in 1959, and on Broadway four years later, in the revival of Oscar Wilde's *The Importance of Being Earnest.* Mia's performance in *Rosemary's Baby,* directed by Roman Polanski in 1968, marked her Hollywood breakthrough, but it was as Woody Allen's muse in such films as *Midsummer's Sex Comedy, Broadway Danny Rose, The Purple Rose of Cairo,* and *Zelig* that Farrow became a celebrated actress. Known for her marriages to Frank Sinatra, and conductor-composer Andre Previn, as well as a relationship with Woody Allen that ended bitterly, Farrow retains a persona of waiflike delicacy and fragility.

In her memoir, *What Falls Away,* Mia Farrow recalled:

> There were seven children in my family...Michael was the oldest, then Patrick, and I followed as the senior of the ensuing cluster of five.
>
> Mike was so smart that even when they skipped him a grade, he got straight A's. And he was handsome too, an Adonis, people used to say. The girls were nuts about him. I could tell from the way they got all mushy around him, and they called so often that my parents had to get him his own phone number. There was always a bunch of his friends around, tinkering with cars on the driveway, in and out of the swimming pool, with music going, chasing here and there, cutting up—Mike had it all. He's gonna be the president, I used to think, and the topper was that he loved me. I never doubted it.
>
> "How's it going, Mouse?" he'd say, because I was a runt, and I'd

feel my face go all hot and I could scarcely look at him for happiness. The presence of my brother's friends around the house almost chased away lingering tendrils of the dark nights and made the world seem well and happy and safe.

Buddy Foster and his sister Jodie

Starring in the hugely successful science-fiction film *Contact,* Jodie Foster is among the world's leading actresses today. Raised in Los Angeles by a financially hard-pressed mother who had been deserted by her husband, "little Jodie," as she was called, often depended on her siblings for nurturing. Her older brother, Buddy, was a well-known child actor who appeared in such roles as Ken Berry's son in the television program *Mayberry, R.F.D.*

Jodie's own career was launched when, at the age of three, she successfully auditioned for a Coppertone suntan lotion ad. By the time she was fifteen, under her mother's skillful management, Jodie had appeared in more than fifty television shows, including *Bonanza, Gunsmoke,* and *The Partridge Family* and starred in the movies *Alice Doesn't Live Here Anymore* and *Taxi Driver* (for which she won an Oscar nomination in 1976). After studying acting at Yale University, Jodie appeared in a variety of well-received films, including *The Silence of the Lambs, Somersby, Nell,* and *Home for the Holidays,* which she also directed.

In writing his sister's unauthorized biography, *Foster Child,* Buddy reminisced:

> As a baby just home from the hospital, Jodie had the lightest skin I had ever seen, and a perfectly bald head, save for a few little white hairs. From the beginning, her eyes were deep, clear pools of blue. I would sit next to the crib and marvel at her.
>
> Jodie stunned everybody, including her pediatrician, by learning to walk when she was only about six or seven months old, just after our move to Granada Hills. At the end of her first year, she spoke fluently, with an impressive vocabulary. She was precocious in every way, her curiosity and desire to learn unquenchable.
>
> It was mind-boggling how quickly Jodie developed in those years. She was simply the cutest, brightest kid around. Even as a small child, Jodie had her now-famous husky voice. That voice, combined with some of the startlingly grown-up things she said, really amazed grown-ups.
>
> But she was also, in many ways, a typically rambunctious, pesky little sister. It was as though she was trying everything on for size; anything we did, she had to do, too. It was impossible for me to shake her, and she mimicked everything I said or did. "Jodie, shut up," I'd snap, and she'd just flash that smile. It was hard to get made at her with that smile of hers.

Maureen Reagan and her brother Michael

Maureen Reagan is the oldest of three children born to former U.S. President Ronald Reagan. Her mother was his first wife, the Hollywood actress Jane Wyman. The two divorced in 1948, and her father would later marry Nancy Davis, who became the nation's First Lady.

Maureen is currently active nationally on behalf of the Alzheimer's Association, and also recently helped produce a documentary about her father's influential life. In 1945, when Maureen was four years old, her parents adopted an infant son, Michael, who is today a well-known radio commentator and talk show host.

In her memoir, *First Father, First Daughter,* the Presidential daughter reminisced:

> The biggest difference for Michael was that he had an older sibling to teach him the ways of the world, or at least the ways of the Reagan household. He had me to pave the way with Dad, or **Mother,** and he had me to help him get his hands on what he wanted. I knew which strings to pull and which ones to leave alone, and I could explain the differences for him. He also had me to spill the beans that he was adopted.
>
> Now, in my defense, it's not all that unusual for an older sibling to tease a younger one with lines like, "Oh, yeah? Well, you're adopted!" In our case, however, the taunt just happened to be true.

Michael remembers that he came upstairs to tell me a surprise one day—that I was getting a new dress or something for his birthday—and I didn't want to hear it, so I said to him, "Well, I have a surprise for you..." That's when I dropped the bombshell.

I don't think he was mature enough to understand what being adopted meant. My parents weren't keeping the news from him so much as they were waiting until he was older and better able to process this piece of information—but I decided it was time for him to know.

When my parents stepped in to clear up the mess I'd made...I remember listening in on the discussion, and by the time my parents were through, they'd made such a convincing case for adoption that even I went around saying I was adopted for a while. They made being adopted sound so much better than just being born, as I was.

In Michael Reagan's own memoir, *On the Outside Looking In,* he remembered:

> Maureen and I grew up very close. She was pretty, blond, and had a pert nose like Mom's. She was the one person I could turn to when I had a problem. If she was angry with someone, I was angry with that person, too. Maureen was not only my older sister, but she started taking the place of my mother. I admired and emulated Maureen and followed wherever she led.

Iovanna Wright and her sister Svetlana

Frank Lloyd Wright was one of America's most influential and imaginative architects. During a career of almost seventy years lasting into the post-World War II era, he created a striking variety of architectural forms. Wright was renowned for creating and expounding the approach known as "organic architecture," in which buildings are meant to harmonize both with their inhabitants and their physical surroundings. More than two hundred and eighty of his buildings are still standing, including New York City's Guggenheim Museum and the Civic Center in Marin County (California).

Growing up in rural Wisconsin, Wright began his career with the prestigious architectural firm of Dankmar Adler and Louis Sullivan in Chicago. Married three times, Wright helped to raise seven children, several of whom became architects under his tutelage. In *About Wright,* an anthology of personal reminiscences, the famed architect's daughter Iovanna fondly recalled:

> I have never gotten over the unity I felt with Svetlana, my mother's daughter by a previous marriage. When I was three, Svetlana was eleven. Mother kept photographs—so precious to me—of Svetlana and me out playing in the snow together. Maybe those were the real days for me. Svetlana always addressed my father as "Daddy Frank." She was a big help in my life. She had wonderful advice to give, and

had wisdom far beyond her years. It was never as though she were my half-sister. She was my full sister, and father loved her every bit as much as he loved me. She was my only sister—as nobody else ever was.

Sharing Companionship in Old Age

———

Maja Einstein and her brother Albert

Albert Einstein is revered today as perhaps history's greatest scientific genius, irrevocably transforming our very conceptions of space, time, and energy. His brilliant "thought experiments" and insights seemed to come out of nowhere, and initially, German-born Einstein developed his profound, early theory of relativity while working as a relatively isolated, patent-office clerk in Bern, Switzerland. Yet, this Nobel Prize-winning mathematician and physicist also had a little-known "human" side.

In *Einstein: A Life,* biographer Denis Brian related:

> On the rare occasions when [young] Albert mixed with children his age, he was quiet and withdrawn, the onlooker. Relatives thought of him as a dear little fellow who never joined in the other children's squabbles, except to separate the combatants. His younger sister knew the other Albert, the little hellion with a wild temper, and she bore the brunt of his ferocity.

Maja escaped serious and frequent injury because she could detect the onset of his rages—his face turned yellow—and would run for cover. His color change was not a foolproof warning signal, however. Once she barely missed getting a concussion from a bowling ball Albert aimed at her head. The next time his face turned from pink to yellow, either her luck ran out or she wasn't watching. He closed in for the attack and smashed Maja over the head with a garden hoe. Years later, when her brother was a dedicated pacifist and literally wouldn't swat a fly, Maja quipped, "A sound skull is needed to be the sister of a thinker."

As adults, Albert and Maja continued a close relationship. In *The Private Albert Einstein,* their family friend Peter Bucky recollected that:

Probably the one person who was closest to him throughout his long life was his sister, Maja, who outlasted Einstein's childhood, both of his marriages, and even his second son and one of his stepdaughters... When he was next to his sister, one could imagine they were twins, so similar in appearance were they, and they had the same philosophy of life. Thus, when Maja came to Princeton and moved in with the Einsteins, Albert was thrilled. She also added a musical dimension to the house, as she was a fine pianist. Often, the house...resounded to the sound of Maja's grand piano and the accompaniment of Albert's fiddle.

Maja died three and a half years before her famous brother, and that was indeed a sad passing for him to bear. Toward the end, she spent most of her time in the Princeton home, and he would come every night to sit on her bed. There he would read her famous works of history, which she enjoyed, as well as the latest news and other items of interest to her.

Annie Elizabeth (Bessie) Delaney and her sister Sarah Louise (Sadie)

In their recent bestseller, *Having Our Say: The Delaney Sisters' First 100 Years,* Dr. Elizabeth Delaney and her sister Sarah Delaney offered a fascinating picture of American life from their vantage point as the daughters of a former slave. They were born two years apart in Raleigh, North Carolina. Their father, freed by President Lincoln's emancipation, was America's first elected black Episcopal bishop and a college administrator.

Sarah ("Sadie") received degrees from Columbia University's Teachers College and became New York City's first black home economics teacher on the high-school level. Her sister Elizabeth ("Bessie") was the second black woman licensed to practice dentistry in New York State. After retirement, they lived together for many decades in Mt. Vernon township, north of Manhattan.

In *Having Our Say,* the two sisters alternately offered their lifelong reminiscences. Each offered wide-roaming observations about their extremely close, sisterly bond. Sadie opened the book by remarking:

> Bessie and I have been together since time began, or so it seems. Bessie is my little sister, only she's not so little.
>
> She is 101 years old, and I am 103.
>
> People always say they'd like to live to be one hundred, but no one really expects to, except Bessie...Neither of us ever married and we've lived together most all of our lives, and probably know each other better than any two human beings on this Earth. After so long, we are in some ways like one person. She is my right arm. If she were to die first, I'm not sure if I would want to go on living because the reason I am living is to keep *her* living.

Later in the book, "little" Bessie described their present activities together:

> Sadie and I get a kick out of things that happened a long, long time ago. We talk about folks who turned to dust so long ago that we're the only people left on this Earth with any memory of them. We always find ways to celebrate our memories of family and friends. Why, we still have a birthday party for Papa, even though he's been gone since 1928. We cook his favorite birthday meal, just the way he liked it...for dessert, we'll have a birthday cake—a pound cake— and ambrosia made with oranges and fresh coconut.

Sharing Concern for an Ailing Mother

◆◆◆◆◆◆

Edna St. Vincent Millay and her sister Norma Millay

Edna St. Vincent Millay ranks among America's leading women poets and dramatists. In the 1920s, she personified romantic rebellion and bravado through Pulitzer Prize-winning poetic works like *A Few Figs From Thistles* (which had the memorable phrase: "My candle burns at both ends") and *Second April,* and innovative theater pieces that included *The Lamp and the Bell* and *The King's Henchman.* In her early career, she was an actress and playwright with the Provincetown Players.

Millay's first poems were published in the children's magazine, *St. Nicholas.* Until she left for Vassar College on scholarship, Millay lived with her mother and two sisters in scenic Camden, Maine, and her work is filled with the imagery of coast and countryside.

In March 1922, thirty-year-old Millay while staying at the Ritz Hotel in Budapest penned these words to her sister Norma:

Beloved sister, bless you forever and ever for your letter. If ever a girl needed a letter, I was that girl, and yours was that letter. You see, it put some things straight in my mind that had been a little cluttered before. Your telling me that mother had been sick…made me realize that nothing in the world is important beside getting mother over here with me. Of course, the Russian famine is important, and a few other things like that, but nothing in my life, at least, is important in comparison to this thing.

A possible marriage, for instance, is not important beside it. Anybody can get married. It happens all the time. But not everybody, after the life we've had, can bring her mother to Europe…Besides, any marriage that could be upset by such a circumstance is not a marriage worth having…

Now my mind is clear again, after an aberration that was just beginning to be more than temporary, and I know what I want, and I want just one thing, and that thing is to get mother over here, and I'm going to do it.

Admiring a Sister's Charm

———————

Beatrix Potter and her brother Bertram

As the creator of Peter Rabbit, Jemina Puddle-Duck, and other animal characters, Beatrix Potter ranks among the most famous children's writers of all time. Born into a wealthy Middlesex family, she grew up in Victorian England and was educated at home solely by private tutors. With a love for both writing and watercolor painting, Potter began her influential career in her twenties by sending illustrated animal stories to the sick child of a former governess. These letters about the Flopsey Bunnies, Tom Kitten, Miss Moppet, and their friends were so captivating that Potter decided to privately publish *The Tale of Peter Rabbit* in 1900. She eventually found a commercial publisher, Frederick Warne & Company, which, during the ensuing thirty years, brought out twenty-three books based on the story that made her famous, including *The Tale of Squirrel Nutkin* and *The Tale of Benjamin Bunny*.

In *The Tale of Beatrix Potter,* her biographer Margaret Lane recounted:

> Like most healthy children, she and her brother were not squeamish, and there was a toughness about some of their experiments which would have surprised their parents, accustomed only to seeing them in the drawing-room, or, meekly booted and pinafored, accompanying elderly visitors around the garden.
>
> Beatrix and Bertram decided to make a collection of all the plants, animals and insects they could find...And everything that they brought home, they drew and painted. They sewed together little drawings of birds' eggs, flowers, and butterflies...
>
> The two of them not only drew every natural object they could lay their hands on, they discovered an obsolete printing press, "a hand press with an agonizing squeak," as Beatrix later recalled, and made elementary wood-cuts...In the hope of obtaining grown-up sanction for the new printing business, they offered a few artistic labels for jam pots; but "the ink was so messy it was confiscated." Anything messy, however interesting, was still forbidden, and the best experiments were those that could be carried out in private.

Sharing Family Grief

Jane Austen and her brother Francis

Jane Austen is widely considered the first great female novelist. The celebrated early-nineteenth-century author of such enduring works as *Pride and Prejudice*, *Emma*, and *Sense and Sensibility* was born into affluence and well-educated for a woman of her time. Her themes were friendship, love, and the complexities of human affection. Austen never married, but maintained close relations with her nieces and other family members. In January 1805, she wrote to her brother Francis, a captain aboard the H.M.S. *Leopard*:

> I have melancholy news to relate, and sincerely feel for your feelings under the shock of it. I wish I could better prepare you for it. But having said so much, your mind will already forestall the sort of event which I have to communicate.
>
> Our dear Father has closed his virtuous and happy life, in a death

almost as free from suffering as his children could have wished. He was taken ill on Saturday morning, exactly in the same way as before: an oppression in the head, with fever, violent tremors, and the greatest degree of feebleness...As the following day progressed, the fever grew stronger than ever, and about twenty minutes after ten this morning, he drew his last gasp.

Heavy as is the blow, we can already feel that a thousand comforts remain to soften it...Being quite insensible of his own state, he was spared all the pain of separation, and he went off almost in his sleep...Adieu, my dearest Frank. The loss of such a parent must be felt, or we should be as brutes.

Sharing Humor and Pranks

●●●●●●●

Maya Henderson Angelou and her brother Bailey

When Maya Angelou read her newest poem at President Bill Clinton's 1993 inauguration, it was another landmark achievement in her multifaceted career. The author of numerous magazine articles and more than ten books, including *I Know Why the Caged Bird Sings, I Shall Not Be Moved,* and *Now Sheba Sings the Song,* Angelou has earned both Pulitzer Prize and National Book Award Nominations.

Maya was the second child and only daughter of urban African-American parents. She was sent, along with her brother, Bailey, to be raised by her paternal grandmother, a storekeeper in Stamps, Arkansas. After working with Dr. Martin Luther King Jr. during the 1960s, Angelou gained acclaim as an actress, playwright, and director and has made hundreds of television appearances. She also teaches American Studies at Wake Forest University in North Carolina.

In her memoir *I Know Why the Caged Bird Sings,* Angelou fondly recalled:

> Bailey was the greatest person in my life. And the fact that he was my brother...was such good fortune that it made me want to live a Christian life just to show God that I was grateful. Where I was big, elbowy and grating, he was small, graceful and smooth...His hair fell down in black curls, and my head was covered with black steel wool. And yet he loved me.
>
> When our elders said unkind things about my features (my family was handsome to a point of pain for me), Bailey would wink at me from across the room, and I knew that it was a matter of time before he would take revenge. He would allow the old ladies to finish wondering how on earth I came about, then he would ask, in a voice like cooling bacon grease, "Oh Mizeriz Coleman, how is your son? I saw him the other day, and he looked sick enough to die."
>
> Aghast, the ladies would ask: "Die? From what? He ain't sick."
>
> And in a voice oilier than the one before, he'd answer with a straight face, "From the Uglies."
>
> I would hold my laugh, bite my tongue, grit my teeth, and very seriously erase even the touch of a smile from my face. Later, behind the house by the black-walnut tree, we'd laugh and laugh and howl. Bailey could count on very few punishments for his consistently outrageous behavior, for he was the pride of the Henderson/Johnson family.

Barry Goldwater and his sister Carolyn

Born in Phoenix on New Year's Day 1909, Goldwater spent most of his life in Arizona. Early on, he was attracted to the military and attended Virginia's Stanton Military Academy and later joined the Army Air Corps. Goldwater was a pilot during World War II, and by the time he retired from the Air Force Reserve in 1967, Major General Barry Goldwater had flown 165 different types of aircraft.

Goldwater's political career began when he won a seat on the Phoenix City Council in 1949. Just three years later, he gained national prominence in getting elected United States Senator. Goldwater ran unsuccessfully on a fiercely conservative Republican platform for president against Lyndon Johnson in 1964, but handled the defeat with characteristic humor. Re-elected to the Senate in 1968, Goldwater mellowed in later years and eventually retired from public office in 1992, at the age of eighty-three.

In his autobiography, *Goldwater,* the iconoclastic Arizona Senator fondly recalled:

> There was deep loyalty among family and friends in those days—even among some acquaintances. The devoted attachment among my brother, sister, and me has endured and grown with the years.
>
> When [my younger sister] Carolyn went out on one of her first dates, Bob and I waited up for her. We saw that this guy wanted to kiss her

goodnight on the front porch. I opened the door, walked out in my shorts, and pretended I was "tossing my cookies," gagging and gasping for air. You should have seen this Douglas Fairbanks [type] beat it down the street. Carolyn said she was going to kill me, but I winked and smiled—and she did, too. She knew her brother loved her deeply.

Another time, she smooched with some guy on the front porch, but I waited until she came inside. I told her people get tuberculosis from kissing. She called me a devil, but I gave her a big silly grin, and she came over and hugged me. That was loyalty.

Ruth Ann and Sally Schwarzkopf and their brother
Norman Schwarzkopf

Raised in Trenton, New Jersey, Retired U. S. General Norman Schwarzkopf attained great popularity as commander-in-chief, U.S. central command, and commander of operations Desert Shield and

Desert Storm in the 1991 Persian Gulf War. He continued to command the operations until his retirement in August 1991.

During Schwarzkopf's thirty-five years of service in the U.S. military, he received a master's degree in missile engineering from the University of Southern California and won many awards, including three Silver Stars, three Bronze Stars, and the Presidential Medal of Freedom. Today, he is active on behalf of numerous charitable and conservation issues.

In his bestselling autobiography, *It Doesn't Take a Soldier,* the famous general reminisced:

> My boyhood would have been perfect had it not been for the fact that I had older sisters. I spent most of my young life thinking that my middle name was "Stupid," as in "Here's my stupid brother Norman" or "Norman, you're so stupid."
>
> Ruth Ann, who was born four years before me, was Pop's favorite. He called her "Yan." She had blond hair [and] loved dresses and braids...Sally, who was two-and-a-half years older than I was, was more of a tomboy. Though she played the recorder and read even more books than Ruth Ann, she preferred to play outside. If Ruth Ann wasn't around, she would sometimes pal around with me and my friends, provided she got to be in charge.
>
> They constantly made me the butt of their jokes. One day they tricked me into thinking that Snow White was on the phone. I had a

crush on Snow White—I had seen the Disney movie and I thought she was everything a boy could ever want—so I grabbed the receiver and listened. "What did she say?" Ruth Ann asked.

"She said, 'Number please,'" I answered. My sisters, who had called the operator, thought this was hilarious. They rolled around on the floor, holding their stomachs and laughing uproariously.

Eudora Welty and her brother Edward

A contemporary Southern writer whose novels include *The Optimist's Daughter, Losing Battles,* and *Delta Wedding,* Welty in her eighties has earned increasing literary attention. Over a career spanning more than seventy years, she has also authored children's books, essays, and numerous short stories. Welty has spent most of her adult life in her hometown of Jackson, Mississippi. Drawing heavily upon regional tradition, a fine ear for speech, and precise description, she has won many awards including the National Medal for Literature, the Pulitzer Prize, and the Medal of Freedom (presented by President Carter). In her acclaimed 1984 memoir, *One Writer's Beginnings,* Welty warmly recalled:

I can't think I had much of a sense of humor as long as I remained the only child. When my brother Edward came along after I was three, we both became comics, making each other laugh. We set each other off, as we did for life, from the minute he learned to talk. A sense of the absurd was communicated probably before that.

Though Edward hated to see me reading to myself, he accepted my reading to him as long as it made him laugh. We read the same things over and over, chapters from *Alice,* stretches from *Tom Sawyer,* and Edward Lear's "Story of the Four Little Children Who Went Around the World." Whenever we came to the names of the four little children we rang them out in unison—"Violet, Slingsby, Guy, and Lionel!" And fell over. We kept this up at mealtimes, screaming nonsense at each other. My mother would warn us that we were *acting* the fool and would very shortly be asked to leave the table. She wouldn't call one of us a fool, or allow us to do it either. "He who calleth his brother a fool," she'd interrupt us, "is in danger of hell fire." I think she never in her life called anyone a fool, though she never bore one gladly, but she *would* say, "Well, it appears to me that Mrs. So-and-So is the least bit *limited*."

Sharing Imaginative Play

◆◆◆◆◆◆

Jorge Luis Borges and his sister Norah

Argentina's Nobel Prize–winning author was born and raised in a Buenos Aires suburb. His father, a civil service attorney and part-time psychology teacher and writer, had a huge library at home, and encouraged his children to read a wide variety of books. The Borges family included British ancestry, and Jorge learned English before he learned Spanish. After moving to Geneva, Switzerland, during his teenage years, he resettled in Buenos Aires in 1921 and, as a founder of the city's avant-garde, began writing poetry, essays and literary journals.

Following a severe head wound that nearly left him dead in 1938, Borges wrote increasingly powerful dreamlike and fantastic stories. After the Peron dictatorship ended in 1955, Borges won many Argentine honors including directorship of its library. By this time, he was stricken with total, congenital blindness, a condition that forced

Borges to abandon the writing of long texts and to begin dictating short pieces to his mother, friends, or secretary. Through his influence, Latin-American literature gained considerable worldwide popularity.

In *Jorge Luis Borges, a Literary Biography,* Emir Monegal recounted:

> For the better part of his childhood, Georgie had an accomplice. It was his sister, Norah, two years his junior...In Georgie's emotional experience, Norah was very important. For some fifteen years, they shared everything.
>
> They shared love, dreams, terrors. If Georgie was older, Norah had a more determined character. She did not inherit the Borges blindness. On the contrary, her eyes were enormous, as if slightly bewildered by the world's profusion of shapes and colors. In the extant photographs of their childhood, Norah's eyes are strong and inquisitive, a petulant smile on her lips, while Georgie's eyes are dreamier, more sensitive.
>
> Norah was destined to become a painter and a draftswoman, and in her works, she leaves testimony of the familial world she shared with her brother. Her paintings and drawings offer an almost [childlike] vision of that world, as if her eyes remember the garden only before the Fall. As their mother later recalled, "He was shy, extremely introverted. He adored his sister, and they both invented an infinite number of extraordinary games. They never quarreled and they were always together before Georgie found in Switzerland some schoolmates."

Jane Bowles and her cousin Mary Jane Shour

Jane Bowles has been called by John Ashbury "one of the finest writers of modern fiction in any language." Francine du Plessix Gray has placed her alongside Colette, Doris Lessing, and Jean Rhys as "one of the twentieth century's novelists who have written most poignantly about modern women [striving for] independence."

Author of the novel *Two Serious Ladies,* the play *In The Summer House,* and many short stories, Bowles grew up in a well-to-do Jewish family in New York City and became part of the Bohemianism of the 1940s. After her first ventures as a writer, she married the writer-composer Paul Bowles. They moved to Tangiers, where Bowles' unique allure and talent brought her into the orbit of such luminaries as Truman Capote, Tennessee Williams, Ned Rorem, and Peggy Guggenheim. In 1973, Bowles died at the comparatively young age of fifty-seven, in a Spanish convent.

As recounted by her biographer Millicent Dillon in *A Little Original Sin,* Jane was very close as a youngster with her first cousin, Mary Jane Shour. Older than Jane by just two weeks, Mary Jane Shour was to marry four times, the first time at seventeen. Starting in 1950, she began to write flippant articles with titles like "Blueprint for a Divorce: How to Get a Husband" and "The Care and Feeding of Millionaires" for *Esquire* magazine.

In her papers, Mary Jane left behind this tantalizing, unfinished fragment about Jane and herself as children during the 1920s:

...there was little of the romantic about Jane. It was in my breast that the fairy tales about princesses and evil godmothers and incredibly handsome young princes-in-disguise dwelt. Jane would have none of it.

The people in Jane's dreams were earthy and had nothing to do with Jane. In them, there was always some wretched old man with a pipe and Troubles. Sometimes the Trouble took the form of a certain fish the [hero] had spent a lifetime trying to lure from its watery home. She wove fanciful tales about the old man and his fish, strange, primly outrageous tales, but never in one of them did he catch his prey.

I'm trying to make you see my cousin as I knew her. A wild, small creature with pixie's eyes and a determinedly unhealthy look: a fey sort of person who works just as hard at her lunacies as the rest of us do trying to keep on the mundane side...

The games we played as children had nothing to do with toys. The only props we ever needed were for the paper-doll games. The rest of the time, we lived in a world of imagination peopled by a succession of beloved characters.

Sarah (Fergie) Ferguson and her sister Jane

Sarah Ferguson, the Duchess of York, has generated huge tabloid sales about her glamorous lifestyle—and romantic escapades—over the years. She married Prince Andrew at Westminster Abbey in 1986 and had two daughters, Beatrice and Eugenie; the couple divorced a decade later. "Fergie," as she's informally dubbed by the English press, worked briefly in public relations and at an art gallery in Covent Garden, followed by a stint at a fine art publishing company. In 1996, she landed a $1.7 million contract as a spokesperson for Weight Watchers, thereby erasing much of her large, personal debt.

Fergie's mother was an English aristocrat who made her society debut at age seventeen before the Queen, and married a well-connected cavalry officer a year later, in 1956. The newlyweds were both excellent horse riders, and their two daughters, Jane and younger Sarah, grew up in equine splendor. In *Sarah, the Life of a Duchess,* biographer Ingrid Seward related:

> The two sisters became the best of friends which.., they remain today. They were used to being together... During the long summer

months of childhood, the two girls played on the closely cut lawns of Lowood House, and while their parents were with the polo crowd at nearby Smith's Lawn, would give elaborate tea parties for their teddy bears with the dogs acting as extra guests. Sarah was always very imaginative and, as soon as she could talk, amused herself for hours in the make-believe world she and her sister shared.

They would take chicken eggs from the nearby farm, find an old tin and make scrambled eggs on the bonfire at the bottom of the garden, pretending they were at their own grand banquet. In later years, they impersonated the riders and horses they saw on television. In their show jumping events, Sarah played the flamboyant Harvey Smith while Jane pretended to be the more gentlemanly David Broome. They built scaled-down jumps to add to the fun of the game...Whole afternoons were spent in this way.

Often, it was so quiet the housekeeper, Mrs. Cole, used to wonder what the girls were up to, until she spotted them on the lawn using part of a washing line for reins.

"It's all right," she would say, "They're just playing horses again."

Kate Greenaway and her sister Fanny

Kate Greenaway was one of nineteenth-century England's most beloved children's illustrators. The daughter of John Greenaway, a London draftsman and wood engraver, she began to exhibit drawings at the age of twenty-two, and her first published pictures appeared in such magazines as *Little Folks*. Initially, Greenaway achieved fame for her Christmas cards, valentines, and magazine sketches. She produced her first successful book, *Under the Window* in 1879, quickly followed by *The Birthday Book, Mother Goose, Little Ann,* and others.

In 1890, Greenaway was elected to the Royal Institute of Painters in Water Colours, and throughout the 1890s, she exhibited drawings, including illustrations for her books, at the Gallery of the Fine Art Society. Hugely popular for her works, Greenaway had personal charm but was shy when accosted by public admirers.

In *Kate Greenaway,* her biographers M.H. Spielman and G.S. Layard recounted:

> The prevailing notes of her life, she insists, were wonder and delight. How limitless, for example, were the pleasures to be got out of the streets, where, with her younger sister Fanny, she was allowed to roam, so long as she kept away from the forbidden land which lay beyond Wellington Street on the one hand and Barnsbury Street on the other. All else was out of bounds.
>
> Where else could they see such fascinating shops and such rustling, perfumed ladies? Where else such a Fancy Emporium into which you could gaze and gaze forever—until driven away by the owner—at the picture-books and puzzle-maps?
>
> …If variety of entertainment were wanted, was there ever such a

diversity of side-shows as the corner of Wellington Street, by great good fortune just within bounds? By good fortune, because Kate and her sister, being out on parole, never dreamed of straying beyond the permissible limit...The corner was full of possibilities.

Vanessa Redgrave and her brother Corin

Born into an English family renowned for its theatrical talent, Vanessa Redgrave is one of the world's leading actresses. She has appeared in more than fifty films including *Blow-up, The Loves of Isadora, Howard's End, Murder on the Orient Express, The Bostonians,* and *Julia* (for which she won an Oscar). Born in 1937, Vanessa was the oldest of three girls; her youngest sister Lynn also became a well-known actress. During World War II, when Germany relentlessly bombed London, the children relocated to a safer, rural locale while their father, British screen star Michael Redgrave, was away helping in the war effort.

In *Vanessa Redgrave, An Autobiography,* she recalled:

Corin and I were dependent on each other's company for long hours of the day, and for entertainment, we put on plays or invented our own games. There was one in particular, our favorite, which we called The Game. We had begun it in Bromyard, during a long convalescence from measles...Somehow the news on the radio about the American heavyweight world boxing champion, Joe Louis, the "Brown Bomber," and his forthcoming fight with Bruce Woodcock, the British champion filtered up to our room.

Corin and I developed a long saga, in which Corin, the son of Joe Louis, and I, the son (not daughter!) of Bruce Woodcock, swapped inventive stories about the lives of our fathers in the boxing world for hours on end. Perhaps these imaginary fathers made up for our own father's absence, or perhaps it was an expression of the wartime alliance between British and American troops that we had heard so much about...

[Later] we created a new scenario, in which I was the president of the United States, and Corin the vice-president. At any spare moment, in the garden, or on a walk, or at nighttime in the bedroom, we still shared long and complicated adventures which unfolded with endless twists and turns.

Sharing Musical Activities

●━━━━━●

Elisabeth Jolley and her sister Karen

Elisabeth Jolley is one of Australia's most acclaimed authors. She is the author of thirteen novels including *Cabin Fever, The George's Wife,* and most recently, *Lovesong,* as well as short-story collections, drama, and non-fiction works including *Diary of a Weekend Farmer*. Born and raised in England, where she trained as a nurse at the height of World War II, Jolley emigrated with her husband and three children to Western Australia in 1959. She holds a professorship in creative writing at the Curtin Institute of Technology, and has won many national awards.

In a memoir, *My Sister Dancing,* published in an intriguing Australian anthology entitled *Sisters,* Jolley reminisced:

> There came a time in my own life when it became suddenly clear to me that my sister was the one person who had known me for the longest time. With this realization, a number of thoughts followed.

One was that the only person who has ever wanted to hear me sing is my sister. In all the things we have shared—earaches, chickenpox, measles, sweets, toys, books, love, ambition, shame, fear to name a few, our two voices have been the most consistently shared in our endless games carried out in dialogue between the characters in our dolls' houses and in a game called Singing in Turns. Some of the dolls' house characters live on still...

"Let's play Singing in Turns." Often at night, we would sing in turns, or, if confined to bed, each in separate rooms with an illness, we would sing. We sang songs like *Drink to Me Only With Thine Eyes* or *My Bonnie Lies Over the Ocean,* or hymns like *Lead Kindly Light* or *All Things Bright and Beautiful.* [The singer would often make a mistake], but the audience of one was quite uncritical.

Sharing Stimulating Conversation

Simone de Beauvoir and her sister Lousie (Poupette)

Simone de Beauvoir was a leading French essayist and philosopher until her death in 1987. Her outlook closely resembled that of Jean Paul Sartre, a lifelong friend and colleague; the two met in Paris when de Beauvoir was twenty years old and became lovers. Best known for her feminist book, *The Second Sex,* which strongly influenced the 1960s women's movement in Europe and the United States, de Beauvoir produced several acclaimed autobiographical volumes, including *The Prime of Life* and *The Force of Circumstance.* Late in life, she also wrote *Coming of Age,* which dealt forcefully with the topic of old age in modern society.

In *Memoirs of a Dutiful Daughter,* de Beauvoir recounted her happy Parisian childhood:

> I owe a great debt to my sister for helping me to externalize many
> of my dreams in play; she also helped me to rescue my daily life from

silence. Through her, I got into the habit of wanting to communicate with people. When she was not there, I hovered between two extremes: words were either insignificant noises which I made with my mouth, or, whenever I addressed my parents, they became deeds of the utmost gravity. But when Poupette and I talked together, words had a meaning yet did not weigh too heavily upon us. I never knew with her the pleasure of sharing or exchanging things, because we always held everything in common. But as we recounted to one another the day's incidents and emotions, they took on added interest and importance.

...In summer, Papa was very keen on organizing expeditions to the woods at Charville or Meudon. The only means we had of enlivening the boredom of those long walks was our private chatter; we would make plans and recall all the things that had happened to us in the past.

I thought it was a remarkable coincidence that heaven should have given me just these parents, this sister, this life. Without doubt, I had every reason to be pleased with what fate had brought me.

Sharing Theatrical Play

❖❖❖❖❖❖

Lucille Ball and her brother Freddy

Lucille Ball was one of America's most popular actresses for more than fifty years. Her career began in stage dancing; she then moved on to film. Using her comedic talent in such television programs as *I Love Lucy, Here's Lucy,* and *The Lucy Show,* she shattered many stereotypes about femininity and "ladylike behavior": Countless sitcom episodes showed her scheming to outwit her controlling husband, Ricky, and achieve her goals. It's no accident that Lucille Ball became the first woman in America to own a major entertainment studio, Desilu Productions. Yet playfulness was always vital to her character and dated back to her childhood experiences.

In her posthumously published memoir, *Love, Lucy,* the famous actress recalled:

I was eight-and-a-half years old when we all moved into the little three-bedroom house on Eighth Street which held first two, and then three, families. It had a front porch and a back shed, and a small, dark front parlor separated from the front hall by portieres. These were the stage curtains for our innumerable productions as Freddy and I grew up...Many of the inspirations for our stage plays came from the fine productions we saw on summer evenings at Celoron Amusement Park....

Since Aunt Lola had a beauty shop to run, her daughter, Cleo, stayed with us and became our baby...As soon as she could walk, she was added to our "repertory company." I would dress her, make her up, and rehearse her lines with her.

[Because] all the adult members of the household worked, I seldom went anywhere without Freddy hanging on to one hand and Cleo the other. For as jealous as I was of Freddy at his birth, it wasn't long before I'd completely taken him under my wing. Not only was he a levelheaded and hard-working little boy, but he was an amiable coaster in all our homespun productions.

Charlotte Bronte and her sisters Anne and Emily, and her brother Branwell

The Bronte sisters—Charlotte, Emily, and Anne—were famous English novelists whose lives and work are associated with the lonely moors of nineteenth-century Yorkshire. Patrick Bronte, the sisters' father, was a poor, eccentric Irishman who became the parish clergy in the small, isolated town of Harworth, Yorkshire. His wife died in 1821, and the Brontë girls, together with their brother Branwell, were mainly raised by their aunt Elizabeth. With few jobs available for educated women at the time, the three worked intermittently as governesses or schoolteachers, and lived almost their entire lives together at home on the desolate moors. Shy and poor, they occupied themselves with music, drawing, theater, reading—and above all—writing.

Charlotte Brontë is best known for her brilliant, semi-autobiographical novel *Jane Eyre,* based on her horrid boarding school experience and later work as a governess.

As recounted by biographer Rebecca Fraser in *The Brontës,* Charlotte described how, at the age of twelve in December 1828, she and her three siblings created the play *Islanders*:

> One night, about the time when the cold sleet and dreary fogs of November are succeeded by the snow storms and high piercing night winds of confirmed winter, we were all sitting round the warm, blazing kitchen fire, having just concluded a quarrel with [our nanny] Tabby concerning the propriety of lighting a candle from which she came off victorious—no candle having been produced, a long pause succeeded which was at last broken by Branwell saying, in a lazy manner, "I don't know what to do." This was re-echoed by Emily and Anne.

Tabby: Why you may go to bed.
Branwell: I'd rather do anything than that.
Charlotte: You're so glum tonight.
Tabby: Well, suppose we each had an island.
Branwell: If we had, I would choose the Island of Man.
Charlotte: And I would choose the Isle of Wight.
Emily: The Isle of Arran for me.
Anne: And mine should be Guernsey.
Charlotte: The Duke of Wellington should be my chief man,
Branwell: [Heries] should be mine.
Emily: Walter Scott should be mine.
Anne: I should have Bentinck.

Soon they went to bed.

The next day, we added several others to our list of names till we had got almost all the chief men in the kingdom.

Sibling Rivalry

Vanessa Stephen Bell and her sister Virginia Woolf

The older sister of writer Virginia Woolf, Vanessa Bell was a well-known painter and a major figure in London's iconoclastic "Bloomsbury" circle of writers, artists, and social critics. She studied at the Painting School of the Royal Academy. Along with the art critic Roger Fry and the painter Duncan Grant, Bell founded the celebrated Omega Workshops, which brought a bright, innovative palette to the field of interior design. Strong, free-willed, and passionate, she had many romances over the course of her life, but always remained devoted to equally creative Virginia.

In *Vanessa Bell,* her biographer Frances Spalding recounts:

> Looking back on her childhood, Vanessa reflected that any sense of rivalry between herself and her sister was avoided by the tacit agreement that one was to become an artist and the other a writer...Both sisters recognized at an early age the difference in their temperaments, Vanessa appreciating Virginia's wit and cleverness, Virginia relaxing

in the presence of Vanessa's relative maturity and calm good sense.

Virginia's early dependence on Vanessa was reflected in her habit of fingering her sister's amethyst beads and enumerating with each the name of a friend or relative whose place in Vanessa's affections had aroused her jealousy. They spent many hours alone in the small conservatory at the back of the house. Here Vanessa painted or drew while Virginia read aloud or wrote the family newspaper, the *Hyde Park Gate News*...The two sisters also had their lessons together at home, but were sent out for piano, singing and dancing classes, none of which they enjoyed...Vanessa kept pace with her more brilliant sister not be dependence on her wits, but through her strength of character. Even as a girl she seemed to have had an emotional effect on those nearest to her that invited reverence.

Jacqueline Kennedy Onassis and her sister Lee Bouvier Radziwill

When Jacqueline Kennedy Onassis died shortly before her sixty-fifth birthday, she left behind an unforgettable legacy. Certainly, Jackie was admired for her accomplishments as an influential book editor and tireless spokesperson for the arts in the United States. However, she is probably best remembered by her family—and the entire stunned nation—for her quiet dignity in the aftermath of President John F. Kennedy's assassination in 1963.

Though growing up in a wealthy and privileged background, Jackie often found herself competing through adolescence and young adulthood with her sister Lee for desirable friends and social status. There was rivalry; for example, when Jackie was named Debutante of the Year and Lee was not. Likewise, Jackie had graduated from college with honors, but Lee never went to college. In *In Her Sister's Shadow*, written by Diane DuBois, the biographer recounted that a turning-point in their intense relationship finally came:

> When Lee went to live in England [in 1955], the balance in the relationship between her and her older sister shifted. Gone were the days when Jackie would write home to Lee from Paris of her exciting adventures, while Lee sighed and longed to be there too. Now it was Lee's turn to write to her sister from London *of her* adventures, while Jackie opened letters and felt envious.
>
> With Jackie's day-to-day circle of acquaintances made up mostly of her husband's Irish cronies and relatives, she envied Lee her glamorous life with the international set, and when she came to visit her in London, Lee provided her with an entree to people she would not have met otherwise...In just a few short months, Lee had made a rite of passage from being a relatively obscure American girl newly arrived on Europe's shore to circulating in some of the highest reaches of the British aristocracy and international society [and she helped Jackie circulate in that world too].

Teaching the Art of Storytelling

◆━◆━◆━◆

Helena Petrovna Blavatsky and her sister Vera

Born in the Ukraine, Helena Blavatsky gained international fame in the late nineteenth century for her books—still widely read in "New Age" circles—on such esoteric topics as reincarnation, spiritualism, and Tibetan Buddhist mysticism. Traveling extensively in Asia after a brief, unsatisfactory marriage as a teenager, Blavatsky settled in New York City during the 1870s and, with her friend H. S. Olcott, founded the Theosophical Society. In 1877, her major work, *Isis Unveiled,* was published to wide acclaim for its bold synthesis of science, religion, and the occult. Later, Blavatsky edited *The Theosophist* and wrote a variety of mystical treatises including *The Voice of Silence* and *The Secret Doctrine*. Her claims to be a psychic medium were vigorously disputed by the London Society for Psychical Research, and she spent her final years quietly living in India.

In *HPB* [Blavatsky's well-known acronym], her biographer Sylvia Cranston relates: "Fortunately, much of what occurred during the children's growing years was recorded by Helena's younger sister, Vera. At the age of ten, she started a diary, reconstructing the previous years while her memory was fresh. Her diaries became the basis for two autobiographies, *When I Was Small* and *My Adolescence,* and her stories for young people, like those of Louisa May Alcott for American youth, inspired several generations of Russian children."

Vera recalled of her older sister:

It was her delight to gather around herself a party of us younger children at twilight, and, after taking us into the large dark museum [of our grandmother's house] to hold us there spellbound with her weird stories...Each of the stuffed animals in the museum had taken her into its confidence, had divulged to her the history of its life in its previous incarnations or existences. Where had she heard of reincarnation, or who could have taught her anything of [these] mysteries in a Christian family?

Yet, she would stretch herself on her favorite animal, a gigantic stuffed seal, and caressing its silvery, soft white skin, she would repeat to us his adventures as told to her by himself, in such glowing colors and eloquent style, that even grown-up persons found themselves interested involuntarily in her narratives.

Agatha Christie and her sister Madge

Agatha Christie, born in Devon, England, in 1890, was acclaimed as one of the greatest mystery writers of our age. She was educated at home by her mother. While serving as a volunteer nurse during World War I, she began actively writing and published her first novel soon after. With the appearance of *The Murder of Roger Ackroyd* in 1926, Agatha gained major recognition. There followed seventy-five successful novels, twenty-five of them featuring the detective Hercule Poirot. *Witness for the Prosecution, Death on the Nile,* and *Murder on the Orient Express* were adapted for film. Where did such imaginative talent originate?

In Christie's *Autobiography,* the celebrated author vividly recalled:

My sister had a game which both fascinated and terrified me. This was "The Elder Sister." The theme was that in our family was an elder sister, senior to my sister and myself. She was [insane] and lived in a cave at Corbin's Head, but sometimes came to the house. She was indistinguishable in appearance from my sister, except for her voice, which was quite different. It was a frightening voice, a soft oily voice.

"You know who I am, don't you dear? I'm your sister Madge. You don't think I'm anyone else, do you? You wouldn't think *that*?"

I used to feel indescribable terror. Of course, I knew really it was only Madge pretending—but was it? Wasn't it perhaps true? That voice, those crafty sideways-glancing eyes. It *was* the elder sister!

My mother used to get angry. "I won't have you frightening the child with this silly game, Madge."

Madge would reply reasonably enough:

"But she asks me to do it."

I did. I would say to her:

"Will the elder sister be coming soon?"

"I don't know. Do you want her to come?"

"Yes—yes, I do…"

Did I really? I suppose so.

My demand was never satisfied at once. Perhaps two days later, there would be a knock at the nursery door, and the voice:

"Can I come in, dear? It's your elder sister…"

Many, many years later, Madge had only to use the elder sister voice and I would feel chills down my spine.

Teaching Boldness

••••••

Shana Alexander and her sister Laurel

Shana Alexander's journalism career has spanned more than fifty years. The first woman staff writer and columnist for *Life* magazine, Alexander subsequently became *McCall's* first woman editor. Active with CBS News for many years, Alexander appeared regularly on *60 Minutes'* feature, *Point Counterpart*. Her books include *Anyone's Daughter,* focusing on Patty Hearst, *Very Much a Lady,* about the convicted murderer-headmistress Jean Harris, and a memoir, *Happy Days: My Mother, My Father, My Sister and Me,* in which Shana chronicled her famous family: her mother, Cecelia Ager was a star reporter for *Variety* and her father, Milton Ager, was famous for writing songs like "Ain't She Sweet," "Hard Hearted Hannah," and "Happy Days Are Here Again."

In this memoir, Shana Alexander recalled:

Our parents believed in reason and intellect above all things, and their children's behavior must often have baffled them. Sometimes it baffled us. Once Laurel was sent home from kindergarten for having put a pussy willow up her nose. "Now, Laurel," Milton said in his most reasonable voice, "why did you put a pussy willow up your nose?"

"It *fell* up my nose," she replied. He couldn't talk her out of it.

Alexander also recalled that, "[My mother] believed above all that children had certain responsibilities which must not be ducked; to *duck* was her only four-letter-word...

Laurel, the braver daughter, talked back occasionally, me never. Like most kids, she sometimes enjoyed being bad for the hell of it. She led the way in our six A.M. forays through the livings room after parties, draining the dregs from all the cocktail glasses before anyone else was afoot. One night when our parents were out, she broke all the English cigarette holders in half. Another night she threw all our brushes and combs out the window.

"Who did it?"

"*I did it!*" said the defiant four-year-old. Laurel never ducked.

Peter (Cohon) Coyote and his sister Elizabeth Cohon

Actor Peter Coyote (who renamed himself after a mystical vision he had while on peyote) grew up as the son of a difficult, talented Wall Street trader. Beginning in 1964, when he arrived in San Francisco fresh from

Grinnell College, he became involved in the psychedelic counterculture and joined the San Francisco Mime Troupe, a radical street theater company.

For fifteen years, Coyote was active with communal efforts in the Bay Area, including the Diggers, a group devoted to "liberating the imagination from economic assumptions of profit and private property." Coyote has frequently headed the California State Arts Council and is active in anti-pollution efforts. Besides Coyote's numerous television appearances and audio narrations, his more than fifty film credits include *E.T., The Extraterrestrial; Bitter Moon;* and most recently, *Sphere.*

In his memoir, *Sleeping Where I Fall,* the iconoclastic actor recalled the influence of his younger sister, "Muffett":

> I must also acknowledge my own childhood cowardice, because my younger sister, though exempted from wrestling lessons (and other expectations to the point of neglect sometimes), was psychologically immune to our father Morris' threats. When he rampaged through the house, smashing things, Elizabeth would stand up to him. Once, enraged by her pluck, he jerked her off her feet by her shirtfront, lifting her face level to his own. She stuck her tiny mug in his and said, "Go ahead, hit me. I'll sue ya!"
>
> Had I done that, the retribution would have been unimaginable, but Morris was first taken aback, then roared at her fierce bantam-hen spirit, and ended by kissing her extravagantly.

Teaching Cooperation

●━●━●━●━●

Heather Whitestone and her sisters Melissa and Stacey

Children with severe hearing loss often struggle to achieve what their non-impaired peers take for granted, and the former Miss America Heather Whitestone is no exception. As an infant, she nearly died during a comatic illness, and suffered profound hearing damage in both ears as a result. But Heather's mother, Daphne Grey, refused to accept for her daughter what seemed like inevitable limitations. In her inspirational book, *Yes, You Can, Heather! The Story of Heather Whitestone, Miss America 1995,* Daphne described how she studied "thousands of practical little insights, ideas, and techniques I could put into practice to help foster communication with Heather"—and then wisely enlisted Heather's two sisters, Melissa and Stacey, as vital partners in healing:

> Heather's training soon became an everyday part of the White-stone family lifestyle. We all took part. Stacey and Melissa were never

just Heather's sisters; they were also her teachers. And Heather's instinctive drive to keep up with and mimic her sisters motivated much of her continuing development.

While she was for the most part a cheerful and cooperative little girl, Heather's loss of hearing had done nothing to decrease the streak of occasional stubbornness she'd exhibited since birth. Sometimes she could be so bullheaded in her refusal to cooperate that I had to resort to a little trickery to bring her around. Knowing that the desire to imitate her sisters could sometimes be even stronger than her stubbornness, I would actually involve my older daughters in the plot.

I'd make an elaborate show of asking [Stacey and Melissa] to do what I wanted Heather to do. They, like Heather, would refuse—for a very short time. Then I'd scold them vociferously and they'd quickly obey, which would often prompt Heather to do likewise. Stacey and Melissa thought it great fun when I gave them occasional license to be naughty and disobey Mummy—even if it was just play acting.

I very quickly realized how fortunate I was that Heather was a third child. How much harder my challenge would have been without Stacey's and Melissa's help.

Teaching to Fight Prejudice

▬▬▬▬▬▬

Margaret Thatcher and her sister Muriel

Margaret Thatcher was the first woman to serve as England's prime minister. Born into a middle-class, politically involved family in Lincolnshire, she studied at Oxford University, worked as a research chemist after World War II, then shifted to a career in law and politics while raising two children. She became Conservative Party leader and prime minister in 1975 and for fifteen years politically headed her nation; her three-term tenure marked her as England's longest-serving prime minister in the twentieth century.

Ten years after resigning her post due to party infighting about her stringent economic policies, Thatcher was made a life peer by England's royalty. She continues to advance her political views through public speaking, writing, and a private foundation named for her. In her autobiography, *The Path to Power,* Thatcher reminisced about an important phase of her childhood:

My family understood particularly Hitler's brutal treatment of the Jews. At school, we were encouraged to have foreign pen-friends....My sister, Muriel, had an Austrian Jewish penfriend called Edith. After the *Anschluss* [German take-over of Austria] in March 1938, Edith's father, a banker, wrote to mine asking whether he could take his daughter, since he very clearly foresaw the way events were leading.

She was seventeen, tall, beautiful, well-dressed, evidently from a well-to-do family, and spoke good English. She told us what it was like to live as a Jew under an anti-semitic regime. One thing Edith reported particularly stuck in my mind: the Jews, she said, were being made to scrub the streets.

We wanted to see Hitler's wickedness end, even by war if that proved necessary. From that point of view, Munich was nothing to be proud of. We knew too that by the Munich Agreement, Britain had complicity in the great wrong that had been done in Czechoslovakia.

When fifty years later as Prime Minister, I addressed the Federal Assembly in Prague and told them: "We failed you in 1938 when a disastrous policy of appeasement allowed Hitler to extinguish your independence. Churchill was quick to repudiate the Munich Agreement, but we still remember it with shame."

Teaching Independent-Mindedness

━━━━━━

David Brinkley and his sister Margaret

Television journalist David Brinkley retired in 1998 after more than thirty years behind the camera. Among the most recognizable faces—and voices—of television news, Brinkley grew up in Wilmington, North Carolina, and was educated at the University of North Carolina and Vanderbilt University. His career as a disseminator and interpreter of the news began early: while still in high school, he wrote for his hometown paper, the *Wilmington Morning Star*.

Brinkley gained national exposure by covering President Franklin D. Roosevelt for NBC, and served as a White House correspondent until he and Chet Huntley launched their nightly news program, *The Huntley-Brinkley Report* in 1956. Offering a wry, somewhat folksy perspective on national and world events, Brinkley offered a unique style. In its fourteen years, the duo won every major broadcasting award and became a model for many other programs. Brinkley subsequently co-anchored *NBC Nightly News* with John Chancellor, then joined ABC for *This Week With David Brinkley,* soon delivering the largest audience in the genre.

In his memoir, *11 Presidents, 4 Wars, 22 Political Conventions, 1 Moon Landing, 3 Assassinations, 2,000 Weeks of News and Other Stuff on Television, and 18 Years of Growing Up in North Carolina,* Brinkley humorously recalled about his childhood:

> In her early years, when my mother, whom we called Mamma, invited friends to [our home] for Sunday dinner, served in midafternoon, usually there was a Presbyterian minister or two being served chicken or two. In addition to the usual bustling around in the kitchen and dining room, there was one more detail to be attended to. My older sister, Margaret, then about five, refused to sit at the table with adult guests or with any adults at all. She hated the smell of their tobacco smoke and found their conversations boring. She asked for, and was given, nursery-sized furniture, a small table and chair to be placed under the dining table.
>
> The adults sat at the dining table, and Margaret sat under it, out of sight. As the adults ate and talked, suddenly and seemingly out of nowhere came a child's voice asking her mother to lean down and hand her something from the table or asking what she should wear to school tomorrow. Family friends were accustomed to this Gothic oddity, but to newcomers it was so bewildering and somehow

upsetting that they found it difficult to converse. A few made excuses and left early.

Theodore Dreiser and his sister Janet

Theodore Dreiser was one of America's most important early twentieth-century writers, pioneering in the naturalist approach. His most widely-known novels include *Sister Carrie, Jenny Gerhardt,* and *An American Tragedy.* Success came slowly to Dreiser, who was born as the second youngest in a Terra Haute, Indiana family that would number ten children. He supported himself as a magazine journalist before achieving lasting literary fame in the mid-1920s. Dreiser was controversial in his own time for writing frankly about sex and other issues. His later-celebrated first novel, *Sister Carrie,* portrayed a small-town, Midwestern young woman who moves to Chicago, and then New York City, where she becomes a Broadway star.

In his autobiography entitled *Dawn,* the influential novelist recalled:

My sister Janet was the cause of considerable worry to my mother…[and]…she was charged by my father with being loose and in need of watching. Bad girl! The endless palaver in regard to that! Whether or not she was, I have no way of knowing, but she gave a bad impression to one as strait-laced as my father. Essentially and in the long run, Janet proved to be one of the best of wives and mothers, sacrificing more for her children than is within the capacity of most women of my kin.

I also tried talking to this sister once concerning this period of her life, trying to piece out the few general facts which I recalled of her and the others.

"What were you?" I asked. "How were you using your time? What were you thinking?"

"Clothes! Clothes and men!" was her reply. "I don't know whether it was because we were poor or because father was so inconsistent on the Catholic faith, but I was wild for anything that represented the opposite of what I had been taught.... When I liked a man, it was easy enough to go with him—it was fun—there really wasn't anything wrong with it that I could see. Aside from the social scheme [that] people seem to want, I don't even now see that it was."

Dreiser ended this dialogue with his sister—and the entire chapter— by wittily declaring, "At this point, I am sure any self-respecting moralist will close this book once and for all!"

Teaching a Life Hobby

———

Josefine Freud and her sister Anna

The youngest daughter of the Austrian physician Sigmund Freud, Anna Freud became one of the world's leading psychological thinkers about children. She grew up devoted to her famous father and after teaching elementary school for several years, decided to enter pediatric medicine. While serving as chairperson of the Vienna Psychoanalytic Society, she published her first professional paper in 1927, on her approach to children's emotional growth. Anna cared for her father at home during his declining years, then escaped with him from Nazi-dominated Austria to England in 1938, a few months prior to his death.

After World War II ended, Anna Freud founded and directed the Hampstead Child Therapy Course and Clinic in London for thirty-five years. In this position, she had international influence and pioneered in treating the emotional problems of adolescents. Her influential books included *Young Children in Wartime, Infants Without Families,* and *Normality and Pathology in Childhood.*

In *Anna Freud,* biographer Elisabeth Young-Bruehl recounted this childhood anecdote:

> The *Kinderfrau* ["Little Homemaker"], Josefine, taught Anna to knit so that she could participate in the family knitting circle, which included all the females in the house. The circle was headed up by Aunt Minna, the most spectacular producer, who had taught both Mathilde and Sophie Freud. But Anna felt that her own work was worth little praise, particularly in comparison to Sophie's. And Sophie flatly declared that Anna was not good at knitting—a remark that her little sister remembered for the rest of her life.
>
> Still, Anna persisted in knitting to such an extent that her parents had to ask her—without success—to spend less time at it. "When I was a little girl and had a new [knitting] project, I had to start it once," Anna told a friend later in life. "I have not lost that enthusiasm. My mother tried to moderate this habit, but she was not entirely successful. I am still the same."
>
> Sigmund Freud also tried to moderate what he called [his daughter's] "passionate excesses," but his entreaties resulted only in a conversion: she took up weaving. His admiring efforts to understand [Anna] then brought him to one of his wilder anthropological speculations: that weaving is the one technique historically attributable to female ingenuity.

Teaching Responsibility to Others

·······

Cesar Chavez and his sister Rita

Cesar Chavez was the charismatic founder and leader of the United Farm Workers of America (UFWA), which he established in 1962 to improve conditions for migrant laborers on farms. The group captured the public eye when Chavez organized boycotts of supermarket produce such as lettuce and grapes. Largely because of his directions, the UFWA won its first contracts in 1970.

Raised in rural Arizona by parents who were Mexican immigrants, Chavez knew poverty from firsthand experience. His family became migrant farm workers during the Great Depression, and he and his siblings attended more than thirty public schools while growing up. In his memoir, *Cesar Chavez, Autobiography of La Causa,* the influential labor organizer recalled admiringly:

> [My older sister] Rita was very conscientious about her work.
> Rita was [also] very smart. When she was about ten or eleven, for

example, she learned how to use the Sears catalogue. Because we lived in the valley and Yuma was a small place, my dad bought everything by mail, from horses' harnesses to clothing. Rita became an expert, almost memorizing the pages, and made out the orders.

Then she heard relatives complain about the catelogues. "Oh, they never send you what you want," they said. So she started making out their orders, and they would get exactly what they wanted.

Eventually, they were so many orders, somebody in the Sears office in Chicago started writing letters to "Miss Rita Chavez." We were very impressed. We were even more in awe when Sears sent her a pen and pencil set after learning that Rita was only eleven or twelve.

At school, too, Rita was admired by the teachers. In fact, I was known only because of her. The teachers would say, "Oh, you're Rita's brother," and make all kinds of compliments about her...Years later, she became a notary public and helped people with all kinds of complicated forms like immigration papers and applications for citizenship. Many still come to her now....

Traveling Together

●━━●━━●━━●━━●━━●

Mary Kennedy Fisher and her sister Anne

Over the course of her colorful life, Mary K. Fisher created a new literary sub-genre with eighteen volumes of witty, erudite essays evoking the pleasures of food and places. These included *The Art of Eating, Among Friends,* and *Two Towns in Provence*. Fisher also wrote a novel and a screenplay. Her 1949 translation of Brillat-Savarin's *Physiology of Taste* is considered a classic. The poet W. H. Auden called her "the best prose writer in America."

Born in Albion, Michigan in 1908, Mary grew up in Whittier, California, where her father owned the local newspaper. Attending several colleges including Whittier and the University of California at Los Angeles, she settled with her first husband, Alfred Fisher, in Dijon, France. Over the course of three marriages, she resided in France, Switzerland, and California, living her final twenty years in a place she called "Last House," set in a Napa Valley vineyard north of San Francisco and designed specifically for her own pleasures, including such amenities as a salon for entertaining while bathing.

In a posthumously-published anthology of her memoirs entitled *To Begin Again,* Mary K. Fisher recalled:

> In 1924, we were sent up [as teens] to Palo Alto to boarding school, and when I was a senior, my sister and I were allowed to go several times to San Francisco without a chaperone. We felt like gypsy queens. The first thing we always did was to stop at the flower stand just off Geary Boulevard by Union Square for blossoms for our left shoulders.
>
> The old man pretended to know us and had a magical trick of folding out the petals of a fresh tulip to make it seem as big as a butter plate. We felt infinitely stylish and carefree and silly and even tipsy. Although we did not yet know fully what that meant, we knew exactly where we were, because we had been there before—through those little satchels of souvenirs of the San Francisco exposition, almost our whole lives before.
>
> Anne and I [went to the theater] with a chosen few other students—thoroughly chaperoned, of course—we saw [actors] like John Drew and Pavlova at The Geary and The Curran and the even dustier old place on Powell. We'd really been there before, with Father and Mother and Uncle Evans; now, we always saved our own theater programs to give our own still-undreamed-of children.

Welcoming a New Sister-in-Law
Into the Family

❖❖❖❖❖❖

Christina Rossetti and her sister-in-law Lucy Brown Rossetti

Christina Rossetti was an important late nineteenth-century poet and a leader of the English pre-Raphaelite movement exalting mystical symbolism and art. Like her London-based brother, Dante Gabriel, who was a famous poet and painter, Christina combined a melancholy and self-critical outlook with a lively sense of humor and a perceptive eye. For several years, she was the only woman member of the Pre-Raphaelite Brotherhood, which she formed with her two brothers and five of their artistic friends. Christina modeled for paintings and became friendly with such Victorian luminaries as Robert Browning, John Ruskin, and Lewis Carroll

Published in 1862, *Goblin Market* is one of her most respected works, a major fantasy-poem about a girl's love for her sister. Her other major writings include a nursery-rhyme collection called *A Sing-Song,* and two volumes of religious prose, *Annus Domini* and *Seek and Find*.

Christina and her brother William were not only close emotionally, but also shared intensely an artistic and spiritual perspective. In July 1873, she offered these congratulatory sentiments to her new sister-in-law, Lucy:

> I should like to be a dozen years younger, and worthier every way of becoming your sister; but, such as I am, be sure of my loving welcome to you as my dear sister and friend. I hope William will be all you desire; and, as I know what he has been to me, a most loving and generous brother, I am not afraid of his being less than a devoted husband to you.
>
> May love, peace, and happiness, be yours and his together in this world, and together much more in the next; and, when earth [in our daily life] is an anteroom to heaven—may it be so, of God's mercy to us all—earth itself is full of beauty and goodness.

References

Alexander, Shana. *Happy Days, My Mother, My Father, My Sister & Me*. Garden City, New York: Doubleday, 1995.

Anderson, Christopher. *Citizen Jane, the Turbulent Life of Jane Fonda*. New York: Henry Holt, 1990.

Anderson, Christopher. *Madonna, Unauthorized*. New York: Simon & Schuster, 1992.

Angelou, Maya. *I Know Why the Caged Bird Sings*. New York: Random House, 1969.

Ashton-Warner, Sylvia. *I Passed This Way*. New York: Knopf, 1979.

Backus, Jean L. *Letters From Amelia, 1901–1937*. Boston: Beacon, 1982.

Bade, William Frederic. *The Life and Letters of John Muir*, volume 2. Boston: Houghton Mifflin, 1924.

Ball, Lucille. *Love, Lucy*. New York: Putnam's, 1996.

Barr, Geraldine. *My Sister Roseanne: The True Story of Roseanne Barr Arnold*. Secaucus, NJ: Birch Lane Press, 1994.

Barnouw, David and van der Stroom, Gerrord, eds. *The Diary of Anne Frank, the Critical Edition*. Garden City, New York: Doubleday, 1989.

Barry, F. V., ed. *Maria Edgeworth: Chosen Letters*. Boston: Houghton Mifflin, 1913.

Barry, Kathleen. *Susan B. Anthony: A Biography of a Singular Feminist*. New York: Ballantine, 1988.

Bianchi, Martha Dickinson, ed. *The Life and Letters of Emily Dickinson*. Boston: Houghton Mifflin, 1924.

Birmingham, Stephen. *Jacqueline Bouvier Kennedy Onassis*. New York: Grosset & Dunlap, 1978.

Bredsdorff, Elias. *Hans Christian Anderson, the Story of His Life and Work, 1805–1875*. New York: Scribner's, 1975.

Brian, Denis. *Einstein, A Life*. New York: Wiley, 1996.

Brinkley, David. *11 Presidents, 4 Wars, 22 Political Conventions, 1 Moon Landing, 3 Assassinations, 2,000 Weeks of News and Other Stuff on Television and 18 Years of Growing Up in North Carolina*. New York: Knopf, 1995.

Brockway, Wallace and Winer, Bart Keith, eds. *A Second Treasury of the World's Great Letters*. New York: Simon & Schuster, 1941.

Buckley, Carol. *At the Still Point, a Memoir*. New York: Simon & Schuster, 1996.

Bucky, Peter A. *The Private Albert Einstein*. Kansas City, Kansas: Andrews & McMeel, 1993.

Burney, Fanny. *Selected Letters and Journals*. Edited by Joyce Hemlow. Oxford: Clarendon Press, 1986.

Bush, Barbara. *A Memoir*. New York: Scribner's, 1994.

Carlton, W.N.C. *Pauline, Favorite Sister of Napoleon*. New York: Harper & Brothers, 1930.

Carpenter, Delores Bird, ed. *The Selected Letters of Lidian Jackson Emerson*. Columbia, Missouri: University of Missouri Press, 1987.

Chapman, R.W., ed. *Jane Austen's Letters to Her Sister Cassandra and Others*. second edition. New York: Oxford University Press, 1969.

Chesney, Edna H., ed. *Louisa May Alcott, Her Life, Letters and Journals.* Boston: Roberts Brothers, 1892.

Chevigny, Bell Gale. *The Woman and the Myth, Margaret Fuller's Life and Writings.* Boston: Northeastern University Press, 1994.

Christie, Agatha. *An Autobiography.* New York: Dodd, Mead & Company, 1977.

Coyote, Peter. *Sleeping Where I Fall*, A Chronicle. Washington, D.C.: Counterpoint, 1998.

Cranston, Sylvia. *HPB, The Extraordinary Life and Influence of Helena Blavatsky, Founder of the Modern Theosophical Movement.* New York: Putnam's, 1993.

Cross, J.W., ed. *George Eliot's Life as Related in Her Letters and Journals.* Boston: Houghton Mifflin, 1909.

Darwin, Charles. *The Correspondence of Charles Darwin, Volume 1: 1821–1836.* Cambridge: Cambridge University Press, 1985.

DeBeauvoir, Simone. *Memoirs of a Dutiful Daughter.* Translated by James Kirkup. Cleveland: World Publishing Company, 1959.

Delaney, Sarah L., and Delaney, A. Elizabeth. *Having Our Say: The Delaney Sisters' First 100 Years.* New York: Dell, 1993.

Dillon, Millicent. *A Little Original Sin, The Life and Work of Jane Bowles.* New York: Holt, Rinehart & Winston, 1981.

Donald, David Herbert. *Look Homeward, A Life of Thomas Wolfe.* Boston: Little, Brown, 1987.

Dreiser, Theodore. *Dawn, A History of Myself.* New York: Liveright, 1931.

DuBois, Diana. *In Her Sister's Shadow, an Intimate Biography of Lee Radziwill.* Boston: Little, Brown, 1995.

Edwards, Anne. *Streisand, a Biography*. Boston: Little, Brown, 1997.

Eisenhower, Julie Nixon. *Pat Nixon, the Untold Story*. New York: Simon & Schuster, 1986.

Eleanor Roosevelt, An Eager Spirit. The Letters of Dorothy Dow, 1833–1945. Edited by Ruth K. McClure. New York: Norton, 1984.

Ever Yours, Florence Nightingale. Selected Letters. Edited by Martha Vicintus & Bea Nergaard. Cambridge. Massachusetts, 1990.

Farrow, Mia. *What Falls Away*, A Memoir. New York: Doubleday, 1997.

Ferrell, Robert H., ed. *Off the Record, the Private Papers of Harry S. Truman*. New York: Harper & Row, 1980.

Fink, Augusta. *I-Mary, a Biography of Mary Austin*. Tucson: University of Arizona Press, 1983.

Fisher, Mary F. K. *To Begin Again, Stories and Memoirs, 1908–1929*. New York: Pantheon, 1992.

Foster, Buddy and Wagener, Leon. *Foster Child, an Intimate Biography of Jodie Foster by Her Brother*. New York: Signet, 1998.

Frank, Elizabeth. *Louise Bogan, a Portrait*. New York: Knopf, 1985.

Fraser, Rebecca. *The Brontes, Charlotte Bronte and Her Family*. New York: Crown, 1988.

Gardner, Ava. *My Story*. New York: Bantam, 1990.

Gill, Stephen, ed. *William Wordsworth*. New York: Oxford University Press, 1988.

Ginzburg, Louis. *Legends of the Bible*. Philadelphia: Jewish Publication Society, 1975.

Goldwater, Barry M. *Goldwater*. New York: Doubleday, 1988.

Gowing, Clara. *The Alcotts as I Knew Them*. Boston: C. M. Clark, 1909.

Graham, Katharine. *Personal History*. New York: Knopf, 1997.

Grandma Moses. *My Life's History*. Edited by Otto Kallir. New York: Harper & Brothers, 1948.

Gray, Daphne. *Yes, You Can Heather! The Story of Heather Whitestone, Miss America 1995*. Grand Rapids, Michigan: Zondervan, 1995.

Gregg, E.W., ed. *The Letters of Ellen Tucker Emerson*. Volume 1 Kent, Ohio: Kent State University Press, 1982.

Grinstein, Alexander. *The Remarkable Beatrix Potter*. Madison, Connecticut: International Universities Press, 1995.

Guth, Dorothy Lobrano, ed. *Letters of E.B. White*. New York: Harper & Row, 1976.

Hoffman, Edward, ed. *The Book of Fathers' Wisdom: Paternal Advice From Moses to Bob Dylan*. Secaucus, New Jersey: Carol Publishing, 1998.

Hoffman, Laurel, ed. *The Book of Mothers' Wisdom: Maternal Advice From the Queen of Sheba to Princess Diana*. Secaucus, New Jersey: Carol Publishing, 1998.

Hood, Lynley. *Sylvia! The Biography of Sylvia Ashton-Warner*. New York: Viking, 1988.

Jones, Frederick L., ed. *The Letters of Mary W. Shelley*. Volume 2. Norman, Oklahoma: University of Oklahoma, 1944.

Jones, Samuel Arthur, ed. *Some Unpublished Letters of Henry D. and Sophie E. Thoreau*. Jamaica, New York: Marion Press, 1899. Reprinted by AMS Press, New York, 1985.

Kelley, Philip and Hudson, Ronald, eds. *The Brownings' Correspondence*. Volume 1. Winfield, Kansas: Wedgestone Press, 1984.

Kilpatrick, Sarah. *Fanny Burney*. New York: Stein and Day, 1980.

Lane, Margaret. *The Tale of Beatrix Potter, a Biography*. London: Frederick Warne, 1946.

Lax, Eric. *Woody Allen, a Biography*. New York: Knopf, 1991.

Leamer, Laurence. *The Kennedy Women, the Saga of an American Family*. New York: Villard, 1994.

Levin, Phyllis Lee. *Abigail Adams, a Biography*. New York: St. Martin's Press, 1987.

Levy, Jacques E. *Cesar Chavez, Autobiography of La Causa*. New York: Norton, 1975.

Lewis, R.W. and Lewis, Nancy, eds. *The Letters of Edith Wharton*. New York: Charles Scribner's Sons, 1988.

Macdougall, Allan Ross, ed. *Letters of Edna St. Vincent Millay*. Ross Macdougall. Westport, Connecticut: Greenwood, 1972.

Maier, Thomas. *Dr. Spock, An American Life*. New York: Harcourt Brace, 1998.

Mansfield, Katherine. *Selected Letters*. Edited by Vincent O'Sullivan. Oxford: Clarendon Press, 1989.

Matthiessen, F.O. *The James Family, Including Selections from the Writings of Henry James Senior, William, Henry, & Alice James*. New York: Knopf, 1948.

McCullough, David. *Truman*. New York: Simon & Schuster, 1992.

McCullough, David. *Mornings on Horseback*. New York: Simon & Schuster, 1981.

McElvaine, Robert S. *Mario Cuomo, A Biography*. New York: Scribner's, 1988.

May, Herbert G. and Metzger, Bruce M., eds. *Oxford Annotated Bible*. New York: Oxford University Press, 1962.

Meir, Golda. *My Life*. New York: G.P. Putnam's Sons, 1975.

Meredith, Burgess. *So Far, So Good*. Boston: Little, Brown. 1974.

Modjeska, Drusilla (Editors) *Sisters*. Melbourne: Angus & Robertson, 1993.

Monegal, Emir Rodriguez. *Jorge Luis Borges, a Literary Biography*. New York: Dutton, 1978.

Morris, Sylvia Jukes. *Edith Kermit Roosevelt, Portrait of A First Lady*. New York: Coward, McCann, & Geoghegan, 1980.

Morton, Andrew. *Diana, Her True Story*. New York: Simon & Schuster, 1992.

Mosley, Charlotte, ed. *Love From Nancy, the Letters of Jessica Mitford*. Boston: Houghton Mifflin, 1993.

Myerson, Moel and Shealy, Daniel, eds. *The Selected Letters of Louisa May Alcott*. Boston: Little, Brown, 1987.

Narrative of the Life of Frederick Douglass, an American Slave, Written by Himself. New York: Penguin, 1994.

Nicholson, Nigel, ed. *The Letters of Virginia Woolf, Volume 1: 1888–1912*. New York: Harcourt Brace Jovanovich, 1975.

Oates, Stephen B. *A Woman of Valor. Clara Barton and the Civil War*. New York: Macmillan, 1994.

Peel, Robert. *Mary Baker Eddy, The Years of Discovery*. New York: Holt, Rinehart and Winston, 1966.

Plath, Sylvia. *Letters Home*, Correspondence 1950-1963. Selected and edited with commentary by Aurelia Schober Plath. New York: Harper & Row, 1975.

Powell, Colin L. *My American Journey*. New York: Random House, 1995.

Pyron, Darden Asbury. *Southern Daughter, the Life of Margaret Mitchell*. New York: Oxford University Press, 1991.

Reagan, Maureen. *First Father, First Daughter, A Memoir*. Boston: Little, Brown, 1989.

Reagan, Michael. *On the Outside Looking In*. New York: Kensington Publishing, 1988.

Redgrave, Vanessa. *An Autobiography*. New York: Random House, 1994.

Reid, Robert. *Marie Curie*. New York: Dutton, 1974.

Riley, Glenda. *The Life and Legacy of Annie Oakley*. Norman, Oklahoma: University of Oklahoma Press, 1994.

Robinson, Roxana. *Georgia O'Keefe, a Life*. New York: HarperCollins, 1989.

Roosevelt, Eleanor. *The Autobiography of Eleanor Roosevelt*. New York: Harper & Brothers, 1961.

Ross, Diana. *Secrets of a Sparrow*, Memoirs. New York: Villard, 1993.

Rossetti, William Michael, ed. *The Family Letters of Christina Georgina Rossetti*. New York: Haskell House, 1968.

Schwarzkopf, H. Norman. *It Doesn't Take a Hero*. New York: Bantam, 1992.

Seward, Ingrid. *Sarah, the Life of a Duchess*. New York: St. Martin's Press, 1991.

Spalding, Frances. *Vanessa Bell*. New Haven: Ticknor & Fields, 1983.

Spielman, M.H. and Layard, G.S. *Kate Greenaway*. London: Adam and Charles Black, 1905.

Stallman, R.W. *Stephen Crane, a Biography*. New York: Braziller, 1968.

Stineman, Esther. *Mary Austin, Song of a Maverick*. New Haven: Yale University Press, 1989.

Sykes, Christopher. *Nancy, the Life of Lady Astor*. New York: Harper & Row, 1972.

Tafel, Edgar. *About Wright, an Album of Recollections by Those Who Knew Frank Lloyd Wright*. New York: Wiley, 1993.

Thatcher, Margaret. *The Path to Power*. New York: HarperCollins, 1995.

Tolstoy, Tatyana. *Tolstoy Remembered*. Translated from the French by Derek Coltman. New York: McGraw-Hill, 1977.

Todd, Mabel Loomis, ed. *Letters of Emily Dickinson*. Cleveland: World Publishing Company, 1951.

Turner, Justin G. and Turner, Linda Levitt. *Mary Todd Lincoln, Her Life and Letters*. New York: Knopf, 1972.

Walesa, Lech. *A Way of Hope*. New York: Henry Holt, 1987.

Welty, Eudora. *One Writer's Beginnings*. Cambridge, Massachusetts: Cambridge University Press, 1984.

Wiesel, Elie. *All Rivers Run to the Sea, Memoirs*. New York: Knopf, 1995.

Wood, Lana. *Natalie, a Memoir by Her Sister*. New York: Putnam's, 1984.

Worthen, John. *D.H. Lawrence, the Early Years, 1885-1912*. Cambridge: Cambridge University Press, 1991.

Yeazell, Ruth Bernard, ed. *The Death and Letters of Alice James*. Berkeley: University of California Press, 1981.

Young-Bruehl, Elisabeth. *Anna Freud, A Biography*. New York: Summit, 1988.